Handbook of Printing Processes

by
Deborah L. Stevenson

Graphic Arts Technical Foundation
4615 Forbes Avenue
Pittsburgh, Pennsylvania 15213-3796
Telephone: 412/621-6941
Fax: 412/621-3049

Library of Congress Catalog Card Number: 92-73936
International Standard Book Number: 0-88362-164-9

Printed in the United States of America

Order No. 1333

A catalog of GATF text and reference books, Learning
Modules, audiovisuals, and videotapes may be obtained on
request from the Graphic Arts Technical Foundation at the
address given at the bottom of the title page.

Printed on Williamsburg Offset, 60 lb., Smooth Finish

Printing compliments of:
Herlin Press, Inc.

Product names are mentioned in this book as a matter of
information only and do not imply endorsement by the
Graphic Arts Technical Foundation.

Contents

Chapter	Title	Page
	Introduction	1
1	Conventional Art and Copy Preparation	5
2	Electronic Prepress Production	47
3	Color Reproduction	63
4	Film Assembly	89
5	Image Carriers	107
6	Presswork	123
7	Nonimpact Printing	157
8	Binding and Finishing	165
9	Paper	191
10	Ink	215
	Glossary	223
	Index	257
	About the Author	265

Printer's Dedication

Herlin Press, Inc. is proud to participate in producing the Graphic Arts Technical Foundation's *Handbook of Printing Processes*. We have been a member of GATF for decades, and continue to avail ourselves of the many benefits, products, and services that the Foundation offers. Their technical plant audits, testing products, educational materials, and seminars have helped us to continually improve our quality and meet or exceed our customers' expectations.

As we approach our 60th year, it is our pleasure to donate the printing for a second GATF publication as our way of showing appreciation to them for their continuing efforts in research, training, and education for the printing industry.

Chester R. Miller
President
Herlin Press, Inc.

Foreword

The Graphic Arts Technical Foundation is pleased to introduce the *Handbook of Printing Processes*. This comprehensive text explains all of the production procedures used to produce a printed piece. It discusses the procedures as they relate to the major printing processes—lithography, gravure, letterpress, flexography, and screen printing—and includes discussions of nonimpact printing, binding and finishing, and paper and ink.

Although this text is primarily for students, and professionals who work closely with printing, without being directly involved in production, we also recommend it as a reference for seasoned professionals as it thoroughly and concisely explains principles that may have been forgotten or misunderstood.

Development of this text was a Foundationwide effort with most of the production supervised by Technical Information Group staff. Deborah L. Stevenson, assistant editor, compiled and wrote the text, and Vicki L. Stone, electronic imaging research technologist, and Thomas M. Destree, editor in chief, created illustrations and contributed material for the chapters on electronic prepress and color reproduction.

The manuscript was technically reviewed by outside consultants and GATF staff. I would like to acknowledge and thank John Coburn, Technical Services, Screen Printing Association International (SPAI), for technically reviewing the material on screen printing, and Cheryl Kasunich of the Gravure Association of America, Inc. (GAA), for reviewing the material on gravure. I would also like to acknowledge and thank the following GATF staff for their technical reviews:

Lloyd P. DeJidas	Frank V. Kanonik
Thomas M. Destree	Charles J. Lucas
Brad E. Evans	Raymond J. Prince
Frederick W. Higgins	Vicki L. Stone

Frank S. Benevento
Business Manager, Technical Information Group

Introduction

Graphic communications is a general term that describes the many different industries involved in designing and reproducing graphic images. Graphic communications is pervasive and dynamic. It is filled with color and imagination, and provides infinite opportunities for expressing creativity and capturing history. It is central to communication; without it, we would have to rely on either the spoken word, which is not tangible or permanent, or hand transcription and recording for all of our information.

All printed material falls under the realm of graphic communications. Even if you have never heard the term, or are unclear about the numerous products that are printed, you are exposed to graphic communications and its many capabilities just by opening this book. Printed materials are everywhere, and you encounter them constantly. They include the newspaper you read with your cup of coffee, the package your breakfast muffins came in, and the billboards you passed on your way to work. Additionally, the soft drink can on your desk and the urgent fax from your manager abroad are also examples of the pervasiveness of printing.

GATF divides the printing and publishing industry into seventeen segments, which include the following:
- Bank stationers
- Book printing
- Business forms printing
- Catalog and directory printing
- Commercial printing
- Corrugated box printing
- Financial/legal printing
- Flexible packaging printing
- Folding carton printing
- Greeting card printing
- In-plant printing

- Labels printing
- Metal decorating
- Newspaper printing
- Periodical printing
- Quick printing
- Yearbook printing

Some segments, such as commercial and in-plant, print a variety of products. Others, such as label printers and bank stationers, print a few, highly specialized items. The establishments that represent these segments are of varying sizes, and are staffed by different numbers of personnel who represent a broad range of experience and expertise.

It is estimated that out of the twenty major manufacturing groups in the U.S. Government's Standard Industrial Classification (SIC) system, printing and publishing ranks first in number of establishments with over 60,000. Because it is sometimes difficult to classify some establishments, a substantial number of printers may not be represented in the SIC.

THE PRINTING PROCESSES

Printing has developed from a mostly manual process to a largely automated one. Much of the original machinery and materials used in the prepress area have now been replaced by computer hardware with microchips and removable disks storing all of the information needed to transfer an image.

The basic printing processes are **planography, intaglio, relief**, **stencil,** and **nonimpact printing.** The **planographic** process prints from a *flat surface*. **Lithography** is an example of it. The **intaglio** process has an image carrier with a *recessed surface*. Examples of it are **gravure** and **steel die engraving.** In the **relief** process, the image area is a *raised surface* that projects from the nonimage area. **Letterpress** and **flexography** are examples of the relief process. In the **stencil** process, an image is printed by *forcing ink through a stencil*. **Screen printing** and **mimeographing** are examples of it.

Several **nonimpact printing methods** are currently used: electrophotography (xerography, electrofax, and laser printing), ink jet, magnetography, electrography or ionography, thermal transfer, and others. Of those available, **electrophotography** and **ink jet printing** are the two most popular.

PRINT PRODUCTION

Production of a printed piece can be divided into three main stages: prepress, press, and binding and finishing. Prepress production consists of the most operations, including design, art and copy preparation, reproduction photography, film assembly, and platemaking. Binding and finishing can also include many operations, some are specialty functions like foil embossing and diecutting, depending upon the customer's specifications.

The accompanying illustration shows the general flow of a job and the personnel involved in the three main stages of conventional and electronic production.

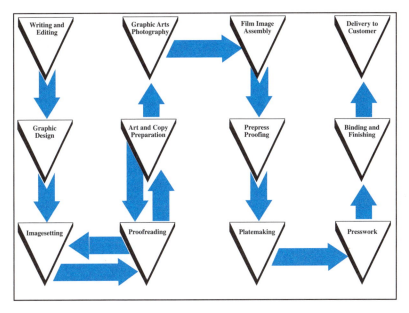

Flowcharting electronic production is difficult as it tends to vary with an individual printer's setup. Electronic production usually requires fewer personnel than conventional requires. Their responsibilities often include several tasks.

Now that you are familiar with some of the uses of printed products and the ways in which they are produced, it is time to become acquainted with the steps that transform a concept into a tangible piece of communication.

1 Conventional Art and Copy Preparation

For the purposes of this book, conventional art and copy preparation along with film image assembly consist primarily of manual operations, although computerized devices are used for such operations as typesetting. Electronic prepress, however, is dependent on the computer for most aspects of production. The chapter on electronic prepress production also discusses electronic systems that output film or plates.

Another difference between conventional and electronic prepress is the number of people involved in production operations. With conventional prepress, each operation is typically performed by a different person. In electronic prepress, one person may perform several different operations, all from a single computer workstation. Hence, conventional prepress can be characterized as being labor-intensive, and electronic prepress as being capital-intensive.

Some jobs are still done entirely by conventional prepress production procedures. Other jobs are done entirely by electronic procedures; and in other cases, portions of a job may be done using conventional procedures, and other parts may be done using electronic prepress procedures.

Planning and Design

Jobs originate in writing and editing and are then sent to the graphic design department. In graphic design, the requirements for the printed piece are discussed, and the best possible presentation is determined. The requirements for the printed piece center around the customer's needs. In determining how a printed piece will be designed, the author/editor or customer informs the designer of the purpose of the piece, the audience for it, the budget, and the deadline for it. These are four very important factors; as all other design specifications will be determined from them.

Purpose/end-use. The use to which the finished item will be put has an important bearing on its design. Asking the following questions helps to determine the end-use requirement:
• Will the design have to compete against others to sell a product? If so, how much impact does it need to have?
• Will the product rely on "soft sell," with a correspondingly restrained design?
• Is permanence required? The life of an advertising leaflet may be measured in days, while that of a book possibly in years.

Audience. The audience for a piece influences the colors of ink and/or paper used, typeface and type style, and the substrate used for the piece.

Typeface critically affects the ease with which text matter is read and assimilated. Typefaces greater than 12 points should be avoided for adults; however, children require larger letterforms for reading and comprehension.

If the piece will be read by an environmentally concerned group, the paper may need to "look" recycled, even though many recycled papers are of excellent quality and do not have the specks and rough textures that many have come to associate with them. The gender of the audience should also be considered when selecting a typeface. Women and men respond differently to type style, size, and design.

Budget. The budget for the job will determine how much time is spent on it and what kind of materials (e.g., paper) will be used for it. For example, the budget determines whether photographs will be printed in full color or just in black-and-white, which is much less expensive. It also determines the number of colors that will be used as well as the printing process.

Deadline. In addition to the budget for the piece, the deadline will govern what can be accomplished with it. If a printer is allowed only a short time to complete a job, the designer will be restricted to producing simpler, less complicated designs.

Once the purpose, audience, budget, and deadline for the piece have been established, the following design considerations can be determined:

Job format. Job format describes the basic size and shape of the printed item. Formats include binding and finishing methods (e.g., hard cover, soft cover, saddle stitched). Planning the format and the quantity needed helps the printer to match the job to the press, as well as to the bindery equipment.

Appearance. The aesthetic aspects of the design include standards of good taste and beauty and design principles. Although appreciation differs from one person to another, consideration should be given to the following points in the search for a commonly acceptable appearance:
- Is the design too complicated or exacting?
- What colors will enhance the design?
- Should corporate colors be used?
- How can a particular theme be emphasized?
- How can design unity be achieved throughout the piece?
- Is there movement through the design?
- Can the color of the paper be used to enhance the design?
- Is there balance in the design?
- Is there a preferred type style?

After discussing the piece with the customer, the designer creates a series of **layouts** that show the customer how the piece will look when printed. The designer begins by making several experimental **thumbnail sketches,** which are small drawings

 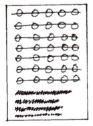 

Thumbnail sketches.

that convey the designer's ideas to the customer. Basically, the designer is brainstorming at this point. Therefore, the amount of detail in a thumbnail sketch is kept to a minimum.

Next, the designer or customer selects one or more of the thumbnail sketches for further graphic refinement. In order to provide the customer with a better indication of the final appearance of the printed piece, the designer then produces a full-size **rough** layout based on the previously selected thumbnail sketch. This layout shows the relative position of the elements of the job—i.e., text matter, display type and headings, diagrams, and illustrations. Display type and headings are usually represented fairly accurately on the rough layout, but text matter is repre-

Rough layout.

sented by a shorthand method, such as the use of parallel lines. Photographs and drawings are often represented by boxes with a large "X" inside.

A **comprehensive** layout showing a higher degree of detail can be prepared. The layout will contain instructions on the type style and size, treatment of the illustrations, colors, and any other relevant information.

Comprehensive.

Typographic decisions, such as type style and type size, are made at this time. Photographs and drawings are also selected.

Type of paper. Paper, which is used as the substrate for the design, plays a major part in the effect of the finished result. Coated stock is used for high-quality, full-color printing, and uncoated stock for general printing. Between the two categories lies a wide range of papers and boards with varying degrees of smoothness, bulk, and texture, in white, tints and colors. Most paper suppliers offer advice and a comprehensive range of samples so that their customers can choose the most appropriate paper for the job.

TYPESETTING AND TYPOGRAPHY

For printing, the characters of written language—letters, figures, and punctuation marks—must be rendered into standardized forms called **type.** While the rendering of each character must have a recognizable basic shape, each particular set of characters (called a **font**) may differ from another set in style, size, or both.

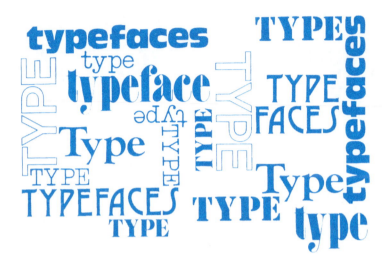

Typefaces.

The particular style of a font is called its **face** or **typeface,** named from the flat printing surface on the three-dimensional type of letterpress. The design of a face affects the ease with which it can be read, the mood it establishes, and certain special functions that may be desired in special situations: attracting attention or providing emphasis. The design takes into account both the appearance of the individual characters and how they fit together into an overall effect.

A font has a particular style as well as a particular size. Type size is usually expressed in points.

Helvetica Regular
ABCDEFGHIJKLMNOPQRSTUVWXYZ
abcdefghijklmnopqrstuvwxyz
1234567890
. , ; : ” ’ ! ? \ - ( ) { } [ ] + = # @ $ % & * ` ~ ^

Font.

The design and selection of the faces and sizes of types and their arrangement and spacing is called **typography.** The actual operation of assembling type into words and lines in accordance with the manuscript and typographic specifications is called **typesetting.** Originally, typesetting was done by hand, but today, sophisticated electronic systems are used to compose type.

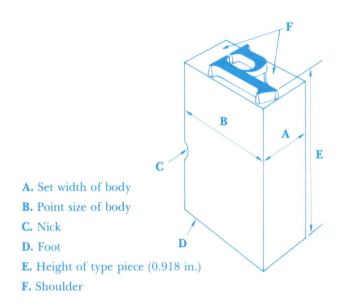

A. Set width of body
B. Point size of body
C. Nick
D. Foot
E. Height of type piece (0.918 in.)
F. Shoulder

Piece of metal type.

Elements of Type Design

The basic unit of type matter is the character. Type design concerns features of the character: weight of the strokes—thin, thick, or varying; kind of serif and how it is joined to the end of the stroke; slope of the character; shapes of the curved elements; and special features, such as the kind of ear on the small "r." These design elements affect the suitability of a typeface for specific purposes.

But type designers also have to be concerned with the overall appearance of the type as the characters are fitted together into words and lines. The first requirement for this, of course, is consistency of style, with respect to the features mentioned above, from character to character. Another consideration is the space between one character and the next. For metal or other three-dimensional types set side by side, this space between letters is the difference between the overall width of the character and the width of the **type body** on which the character is carried. Thus, basic letterspacing is part of the type design. With phototypesetting and imagesetting, the operator can increase or decrease the default letterspacing by entering the proper commands.

This paragraph is set with fourteen (14) points of line spacing. This paragraph is set with fourteen (14) points of line spacing.

This paragraph is set with sixteen (16) points of line spacing. This paragraph is set with sixteen (16) points of line spacing.

This paragraph is set with eighteen (18) points of line spacing. This paragraph is set with eighteen (18) points of line spacing.

Examples of different line spacing.

One problem is that the visual space between characters is affected by the shapes of the adjacent sides of characters. Some combinations of side-by-side letters with normal spacing fit better than others. The early designers improved many of the problem combinations by designing two or more characters together on one type body, a combination called a **ligature.** A few of these, such as "ff" and "ffl" are still present in some fonts.

Sometimes portions of such characters as an italic "f" were made to project beyond the type body to permit overlapping an adjacent letter. A projecting part of this kind was called a **kern.** With the advent of phototypesetting, the term **kerning** was extended to the practice of achieving similar results electronically by reducing the normal letterspacing.

The letters at the right have been kerned.

The Nomenclature of Type

Although machine-setting has largely replaced handsetting and two-dimensional type has largely replaced three-dimensional, the traditions, terminology, and principles of typography evolved from the centuries-old system of handset type. For example, the terms "uppercase" and "lowercase" letters originated from the positions occupied by the capitals and small letters in the typecase. The practice of increasing the spacing between type lines by inserting thin strips of lead is called **leading.** The term "leading" is also often applied to the control of interline spacing in phototypesetting, although **line spacing,** meaning the distance in points from the baseline of one line of type to the baseline of the next line of type, is the preferred term. Many other standard typographical terms originated in reference to the individual handset types.

Type is available for every letter, numeral, or other symbol that is used in graphic communications, and these letters and symbols appear in a great number of designs and sizes.

Type characters. Most fonts include **uppercase** (capital) letters and **lowercase** (small) letters. Although different fonts look different, they have several similarities.

The height of the main element of a lowercase letter is called its **x-height.** The lower boundary of the x-height is the **baseline.** All letters rest on this imaginary line. Modern typesetters are designed so that all characters on a line, regardless of their size, rest on the baseline.

Any part of a lowercase character that rises above the upper boundary of the x-height is called an **ascender.** Similarly, any part of a lowercase letter that drops below the baseline is called a **descender.** The height of a capital letter, or **cap height,** usually extends from the baseline to ascender height.

Some typefaces are designed with short cross-strokes **(serifs)** that project outward from the main strokes (stems) at

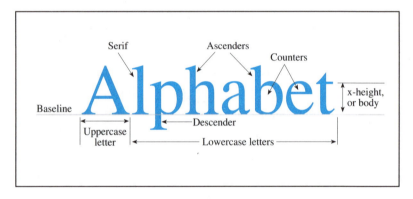

Nomenclature of type.

the top and bottom of the letter. Letters without serifs are called **sans serif.** A sans serif typeface appears more streamlined and simple when compared to a typeface with serifs.

Type family. A typeface with vertical main strokes is called a **roman** typeface. If a typeface's main strokes are slanted to the right of vertical, the typeface is called **italic**. (With some modern digital typesetters and imagesetters, a roman typeface can be electronically angled away from the vertical, producing "pseudo-italic.") Most typefaces are available in roman and italic versions. A roman typeface is more suitable for reading material, while the italic typeface is used to emphasize a word or phrase.

A **type family** consists of all of the variations based upon a particular typeface. Most type families have at least four variations: regular roman, regular italic, bold roman, and bold italic. A **bold** typeface has heavier letter strokes than the regular version. Other variations are also possible. A light typeface has thinner letter strokes than the regular version. With a **condensed** or **expanded** typeface, the character width would vary from the regular typeface. Many modern digital typesetters and imagesetters are able to electronically condense or expand regular typefaces; however, the effect can be overdone.

Helvetica Helvetica **Helvetica**

Helvetica type: 20-pt. normal, condensed 20%, expanded 20%.

Type font. A complete assortment of characters of one size and style of typeface—including capitals, small capitals, lowercase letters, numerals, ligatures, and punctuation marks—is called a **font** of type.

A font of type usually contains a sufficient assortment of characters for setting ordinary composition, such as newspapers, magazines, and other nontechnical material. In some cases, a "pi" font must be used in conjunction with a main font to permit the setting of special characters, such as superior and inferior characters, mathematical symbols, and accented characters for certain languages.

Type series. Most typefaces used in metal composition were made in a wide range of sizes known as a **series.** Generally, a type series in metal composition would begin at a 6-point size and go up to 36-point or in some cases as large as 96-point type. A typical series might have the following point sizes: 6, 7, 8, 10, 12, 14, 18, 24, 36, 48, 60, and 72.

In phototypesetting and imagesetting, depending on the machine, the type series could range from 4- to 128-point type (or larger) in ¼-point or smaller increments.

The point system. The term "point" is derived from the American point system. This system of measurement is used in most English-speaking countries. The point system has two units of measurement: points and picas. There are 12 points in one pica and 6 picas in 1 in., or 72 points in 1 in. (Actually, 6 picas are not exactly equal to 1 in.; they measure 0.99576 in.) Body size of metal types is specified in points, such as 10-point Bodoni. A pica type is 12 points, and agate type—used in newspaper ads—is 5½ points. There are 14 agate lines to a column inch. This is the measurement used to calculate the space occupied by advertisements in newspapers.

Large wood type used for posters is expressed in pica lines. For example, 10-line type would be 10 picas in height. **Line length** is also specified in picas, such as an 18-pica line length.

A ruler called a **line gauge** is commonly used to measure line lengths and line spacing. Scaled in picas and points for a typographer's use, a typical line gauge has seven or more scales in various increments, such as 6, 7, 8, 9, 10, 11, 12, 13, and 15 points.

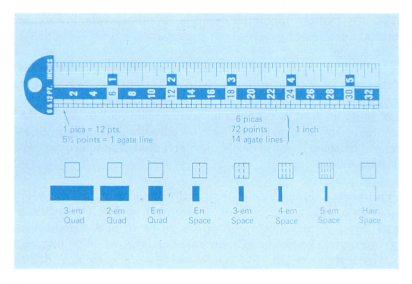

Line gauge.

Line gauges come in different sizes, materials, and configurations and may include other scales, such as inches.

Point size or body size. The height of a character font in metal composition is called **body size** or **point size** and is expressed in typographic points. The measure of the height is slightly more than the distance from the highest ascender to the lowest descender of the characters in the font. It must be emphasized that, although different type designs may have the same body size, the size of the faces will appear different because of the difference in the x-height and lengths of the ascenders and descenders.

In phototypesetting and imagesetting, it is difficult to measure point size because the characters are no longer carried on the face of metal type. Instead, a printed or typeset sample is compared with type of the same typeface in a specimen book. A **specimen book** consists of alphabets of different typefaces in a variety of point sizes. A less accurate method is to measure the distance from the ascender to the descender of adjacent characters. Depending on type characteristics, the measurement might be accurate or it could be off several points, as would happen if a 60-point typeface had extremely short ascenders or descenders.

Modern typesetters and imagesetters allow more than one type style and/or type size on one line (intra-line mixing) or in one job (inter-line mixing).

Basic Typographic Forms

Type may appear in various positions on a printed page relative to the left or right margins or the center of a page

The type in the accompanying illustration is set **justified,** which means that each line of text aligns with both the left- and right-hand margins. Most newspapers, magazines, and books are typeset in this manner. Justified type is usually, but not always, set with end-of-line hyphens. (**Hyphenation** is the process of using hyphens to divide words that are too long to fit on the remaining line measure. **H&J** is an abbreviation for type that is hyphenated and justified.) Short lines of type justified without hyphenation usually have excessively large amounts of word spacing. In fact, with any text that is set justified, the word spacing from one line to the next usually varies.

Another popular method of setting type is the **flush left** format. In this format, copy aligns only at the left margin; the right

In the course of developing the GATF/LTF Society of Fellows Historic Display, a sizable body of GATF contributions to the growth and development of the graphic communications industries has emerged. These rare and historic documents as well as prototype technology will be showcased in the permanent display, housed at GATF international headquarters in Pittsburgh, Pa. A gift to GATF, its members, and the industry, the GATF/LTF Historic Display was funded by a contribution from the GATF Society of Fellows Discretionary Fund.

    In addition, individual members of the GATF Society of Fellows also donated original documents from their personal collections and/or offered personal recollections of the developments to be included in the display. From the most recent to those dating back to GATF's predecessor, the Lithographic Technical Foundation (LTF),

Justified type.

In the course of developing the GATF/LTF Society of Fellows Historic Display, a sizable body of GATF contributions to the growth and development of the graphic communications industries has emerged. These rare and historic documents as well as prototype technology will be showcased in the permanent display, housed at GATF international headquarters in Pittsburgh, Pa. A gift to GATF, its members, and the industry, the GATF/LTF Historic Display was funded by a contribution from the GATF Society of Fellows Discretionary Fund.

    In addition, individual members of the GATF Society of Fellows also donated original documents from their personal collections and or offered personal recollections of the developments to be included in the display. From the most recent to those dating back to GATF's predecessor, the Lithographic Technical Foundation (LTF),

Flush left type.

margin is ragged. Flush left is also known as **ragged right** and **quad left** (a term carried over from the days of handsetting metal type). In flush left copy, the word spacing is constant from one line to the next. In general, words are not hyphenated in flush left composition unless they are extremely long or line endings are extremely ragged.

Type can also be set **flush right,** in which case the copy aligns with the right margin and the left margin is ragged. This format is used infrequently. **Centered** copy is centered on the line length. With **runaround** copy, line lengths are adjusted to accommodate the shape of an illustration or photograph.

In the course of developing the GATF/LTF Society of Fellows Historic Display, a sizable body of GATF contributions to the growth and development of the graphic communications industries has emerged. These rare and historic documents as well as prototype technology will be showcased in the permanent display, housed at GATF international headquarters in Pittsburgh, Pa. A gift to GATF, its members, and the industry, the GATF/LTF Historic Display was funded by a contribution from the GATF Society of Fellows Discretionary Fund.
In addition, individual members of the GATF Society of Fellows also donated original documents from their personal collections and/or offered personal recollections of the developments to be included in

Centered type.

GATF In the course of developing the GATF/LTF Society of Fellows Historic Display, a sizable body of GATF contributions to the growth and development of the graphic communications industries has emerged. These rare and historic documents as well as prototype technology will be showcased in the permanent display, housed at GATF international headquarters in Pittsburgh, Pa. A gift to GATF, its members, and the industry, the GATF/LTF Historic Display was funded by a contribution from the GATF Society of Fellows Discretionary Fund. In addition, individual members of the GATF

Runaround type.

Spacing

Line spacing. Line spacing in phototypesetting and imageset-ting is the distance from the baseline of one line of type to the baseline of the next line of type. The line spacing for text is typi-cally one or two points greater than the point size of the text. However, optimum line spacing also depends on characteristics of the typeface and line length.

Word spacing. Word spacing is the space between typeset words. The phototypesetter or imagesetter operator has control over the minimum, normal, and maximum amounts of word spac-ing. In centered and ragged composition, the normal word space is used between all words. In justified composition, where the type must be flush with both the left and right margins, the machine will automatically expand or condense the word space or hyphenate end-of-line words to fill up the line measure. If the machine is operating in a hyphenless mode or if the line measure is extremely short compared to the type size, the space between words may be excessive and unsightly.

Letterspacing. Letterspacing is the placement of additional space between characters in a line. In phototypesetting and imagesetting, the machine operator has control over minimum, normal, and maximum amounts of letterspacing. If the machine cannot justify a line by expanding word spaces to their maximum value, the machine will insert space between letters.

    Kerning can be considered the opposite of letterspacing. It is the removal of space from between certain letter combinations to improve the appearance of words.

Markup

Once the editor has edited a manuscript, the designer writes typographic specifications such as format (e.g., ragged right or justified columns), type style and size, line length, and line spac-ing on a clean copy for the typesetter. This function is called **markup**. Traditional markup symbols are easily translated by the typesetter operator into the appropriate machine functions.

The accompanying illustration shows the typewritten manuscript marked up with the following typographic specifications:
- Format: justified with end-of-line hyphenation, set as a single column of type
- Type style: Helvetica
- Type size: 9 point
- Line length: 16 picas
- Line spacing: 11 points

If special characters need to be typeset, they are indicated on the marked-up manuscript. A few examples of these special characters are times signs, minus signs, and degree symbols.

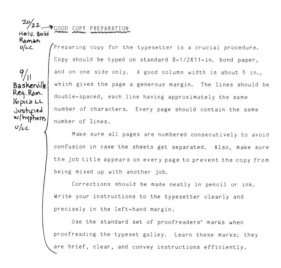

Copyfitting. With many jobs, such as advertisements, the amount of space occupied by the typeset material is very critical. Therefore, a procedure called **copyfitting** is used to make sure the typeset material fits into the space allowed for it on the layout. Copyfitting involves counting the characters, punctuation, and spacing in the original manuscript, and calculating the space that this material will take up in a particular style and size of type set on a certain line length with a certain amount of space (leading) between lines. Since line lengths are usually specified in picas, the designer can refer to the appropriate type specimen book to determine the number of characters in one pica in that point size and typeface.

If the text does not fill the allocated layout space, the designer can adjust any of the four copyfitting variables—typeface, type size, line length, or leading. For most jobs, however, line length is considered a constant. Therefore, to increase the space occupied by the text, the designer can select a typeface that takes up more space (fewer characters per pica), select a larger point size, or increase the line spacing (or some combination of the three) while maintaining the legibility and aesthetics of the piece.

Similarly, if the initial copyfitting calculation indicates that the text will fill more than the allowed space, the designer can select a typeface that takes up less space (more characters per pica), select a smaller point size, or decrease the line spacing, or some combination of the three.

Typesetting

Today, one way to set type for reproduction is photographically, using a phototypesetter or an imagesetter. Although typesetting systems are available in various configurations and degrees of complexity, most consist of a keyboard similar to that on a typewriter, a computer with magnetic storage capabilities, a video display that uses a cathode-ray tube (CRT), and an output unit. The keyboard has both **alphanumeric** and **function keys.** The function keys of a dedicated phototypesetting system, however, include shift and spacing, as well as formatting and editing commands like ragged right, and character and word cancellation.

In general terms, a phototypesetting unit is only capable of outputting type and assorted special characters onto phototypesetting paper using a laser or a cathode-ray tube to expose the paper. If the phototypesetting paper is wide enough, the phototypesetter can output made-up pages without graphic images, such as line drawings and halftones. An imagesetter, as the name implies, can output graphic images in addition to type characters. Imagesetters can also output completed pages, with all type, line illustrations, halftones, and screen tints in proper

AGFA Selectset™ 5000   *Courtesy AGFA Div., Miles Inc.*

position. The use of the imagesetter is discussed in greater depth in the chapter on electronic prepress production.

Type characters are handled in one of two ways on a phototypesetter. Older phototypesetters carried the type characters on photographic disks, drums, strips, or grids, which are inserted into the phototypesetting unit. Newer phototypesetters store the type characters electronically in the photounit itself as digital information, permitting a wider selection of typefaces and sizes. Imagesetters also store the type characters electronically.

The following discussion explains the basic steps in using a phototypesetter. Using the keyboard, the machine operator inputs (rekeyboards) the text along with typesetting commands such as type size, typeface, line length, line spacing, and formatting (e.g., ragged right or justified). The keystrokes appear on the CRT. The text can be rearranged, edited, and corrected on the screen before it is typeset, and words or typesetting commands can be added or deleted. The material to be typeset is stored electronically, often on a floppy disk.

Depending on the capabilities of the phototypesetting system and the computer equipment used by the customer, the job may not have to be rekeyboarded. For example, if the customer supplies the job on a floppy disk, the disk may be usable as is, or it can be converted into a format compatible with the phototypesetting system. If the customer's computer and the phototypesetting system are equipped with modems, the customer can use the modem to send the job to the phototypesetting system. A third alternative to rekeyboarding a job is to use a device capable of optical character recognition (OCR). The OCR machine reads each character on a typewritten or typeset page and stores it in computer memory or on a computer disk.

The next step is the actual phototypesetting operation. The information that is stored on the computer disk, or other storage medium, is transferred to the phototypesetting unit. The photounit then exposes images of the type characters, according to the operator's keyboarded instructions, onto photosensitive film or paper. The output is then developed, like camera film, in a separate processor. The result is a photographic galley proof or a made-up page.

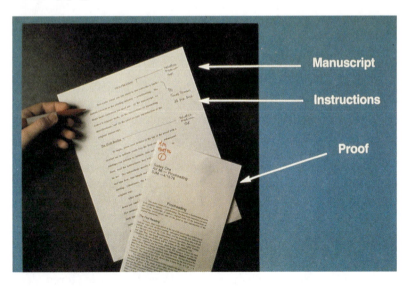

Manuscript, instructions, and proof.

The galley proof will be checked against the manuscript and instructions, and then corrected if necessary.

Proofreading

The output of the typesetter or imagesetter must be proofread, or checked against the original, to ensure correctness. The proofreader uses standard proofreader's marks to indicate errors. The corrections are input by the machine operator, and the new output is checked against the previous proof. This cycle of proofreading and correcting continues until the machine output is error-free.

Proofreader checking typeset galley.

Pasteup

Pasteup is the manual operation of putting phototypeset copy into page form by attaching it, along with artwork, to a strong base sheet. The purpose of the pasteup, or **mechanical,** is to provide copy from which a photographic film reproduction is made for platemaking, or image carrier preparation.

The pasteup artist applies adhesive to the back of the phototypeset output. The pasteup artist has three alternatives for applying adhesive: a **pressure-sensitive adhesive** can be

Proofreaders' Marks

⊙	Period or full point	﹏﹏	Set in boldface type
⌃⁊ ⁊	Comma	Bf	Boldface type (in margin)
/=/ /-/	Hyphen	≡≡≡	Capitalize material
⁊/	Semicolon	cap	Capitalization (in margin)
⌵	Apostrophe		
!/	Exclamation mark	———	Set in italic type
/ₑₙ̄/ /ₙ̄/	En dash	ital	Italics (in margin)
/ₑₘ̄/ /ₘ̄/	Em dash	∧ ∨	Caret
(|)	Parentheses	#	Insert space
⌵⌵ | ⌵⌵	Quotation marks (double)	hr#	Insert hair space
⌵ | ⌵	Quotation marks (single)	☐	Indent one em space
═══	Align horizontally	⌿	Delete or take out
‖	Align vertically	⌿	Delete and close up space
⌐	Move to the left	⌒	Close up
⌐	Move to the right	⑦	Query to author
⌐	Move matter up	.....	Let indicated material remain as it is
⌐	Move matter down	stet	Let it stand (in margin)
✕ ⊗	Broken letters	⋃ ⋂	Transpose material
M	Set in lowercase	tr	Transpose (in margin)
lc	Lowercase (in margin)		

Proofreaders' marks are used to mark both grammatical errors and typos.

sprayed on to the back of the galley, **rubber cement** can be brushed on, or the galley can be run through a **hot-waxing machine.** The use of wax, however, is far more common than the use of pressure-sensitive adhesive or rubber cement.

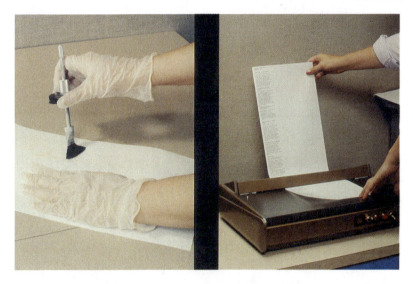

Artist applying cement to copy *(left)* and applying wax to copy *(right)*.

Next the pasteup artist adheres the phototypeset copy onto a stiff paper or acetate **base sheet.** The phototypeset copy is properly positioned, using a T square and triangle for exact alignment, and by referring to the comprehensive as a guide. Many designers use preprinted grids, either paper or transparent plastic, to make copy positioning easier. Paper grids are preprinted using a light blue ink that graphic arts film will not reproduce.

All **line copy**—copy that contains no shades of gray, such as type or line drawings, and does not require the use of a halftone screen to be reproduced—can be adhered directly on the pasteup. Line copy prints solid. Although black type on white paper is most often thought of when referring to line copy, it is actually *any* solid color type on a white background.

The **base art** is the final layout or comprehensive including all type, line drawings, and overlays.

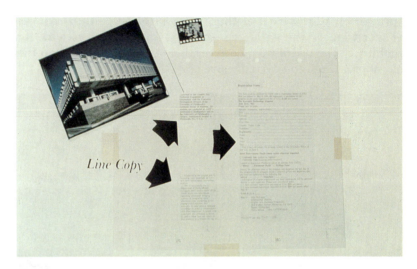

Line copy.

The black arrows in the illustration are pointing to the line copy.

Pasteup.

The artist is pasting down copy (the cut-up, error-free typeset galley) using the accompanying dummy as a guide.

The position of **continuous-tone copy**—copy that contains gradation of tones from light to dark, such as a black-and-white photograph or color transparency—that will be printed must also be shown on the pasteup. Continuous-tone copy, however, is not adhered directly on the base sheet as the line copy is, because continuous-tone copy must be photographed separately.

Continuous-tone copy.

Instead, the exact area in which a photo or transparency is to print is indicated by placing a thin red masking material on the pasteup. It appears as black to the film used in graphic arts photography, so it shows up as a clear opening, or **window,** on the negative when the completed pasteup is later photographed in preparation for making the printing plate.

With some jobs, one image will print over or be reversed out of another on press. Since these images are often printed in different colors, the pasteup artist usually assembles one of them on a clear plastic overlay that is hinged or pin-registered to the base art. The images typically placed on the overlays are ones that will be printed in a color or colors that are different from the base art. If the job is multicolored, two or more overlays may be required.

The artist is placing thin red masking material on the pasteup to indicate where photos or transparencies will print.

The artist is placing a sheet of translucent tissue, through which the board can be seen, over the artboard.

After all the type and line illustrations have been pasted down and the position of photographs indicated with windows, a tissue that covers and protects the pasteup is hinged to the top with masking tape. This is often referred to as a **tissue overlay.**

Instructions to the printer, including where color is to print, are written on the tissue overlay. For the double-page spread shown here, all the type prints in 100% black and the positions of the two photographs are labeled items A and B. The completed pasteup is now called **camera-ready** copy.

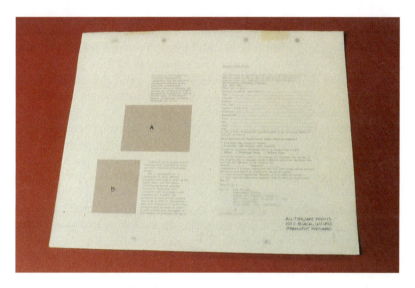

A double-page spread with a tissue overlay that has instructions to the printer.

The camera-ready copy is then proofread again by the proofreader. The designer or pasteup artist also rechecks the photo placement and size. Additionally, photocopies of the pasteup are often given to the editor or client to check. This pasteup/proofreading procedure must be followed for each page of the job.

If the pages are placed in numerical order during pasteup (with odd-numbered pages always on the right), they are called **reader's spreads.** If they are positioned as they would appear when imposed on a film flat and folded, they are called **printer's spreads.**

PREPARATION OF ARTWORK AND REPRODUCTION PHOTOGRAPHY

The two broad categories of artwork—**line art** and **continuous-tone art**—are prepared separately, using different techniques. Different photographic techniques are used to reproduce each category of art, as discussed in the section entitled "Reproduction Photography."

Line Art

Line copy is all copy that contains no shades of gray and prints solid (black or color) on the finished piece. Pen-and-ink line drawings, shading film, and type are examples of line copy. Type reversals are also line copy since the background prints as a solid ink with the type appearing as white. Although such art has no tonal gradations, the illusion of middletones can be created by interspersing thin lines or small dots with white space, such as the cross-hatching sometimes used in pen-and-ink drawings.

Line art to be reproduced by printing should be prepared for maximum contrast; that is, dark solid images on a neutral white background. Large solid areas, especially, must have uniform density. Line art (line drawings) is prepared by a number of techniques. Each technique involves the deposit of a uniform black image on a white background. Wherever possible, line art is prepared larger than its final printed size; a convenient size is usually 25–50% larger. Reducing original copy on camera minimizes imperfections, such as jagged or rough edges, although it does not eliminate them. Conversely, camera enlargements tend to accentuate imperfections in the art.

An exception to this rule is fine-line, detailed line copy. Detailed copy should be prepared in the same size as the printed size because it is difficult to predict how thin the fine lines will become during a camera reduction. Very thin lines may drop out entirely; very close lines may merge into a mass of solid black.

Some of the common techniques used to produce line art are drawing with **pen and ink, charcoal or pencil,** and **brush and ink;** using **shading film;** and making **line conversions or posterizations** of continuous-tone subject matter.

Pen and ink. Most pen-and-ink illustrations are drawn on hard, high-quality, smooth, coated paper or on illustration board, using a ruling pen, technical pen, or crow quill pen.

Pen-and-ink line art.

Brush and ink. Brush-and-ink illustrations are produced in the same way as pen-and-ink illustrations. The brush produces broader strokes with feathered edges. Pen and ink and brush and ink can be combined in the same illustration for a special effect.

Charcoal or pencil. Charcoal or pencil illustrations can create the illusion of continuous-tone copy. Highlight areas are created by applying light pressure to the charcoal or pencil. Shadow areas are produced with heavier pressure. But the marks must still be discernible as distinct dark lines or areas varying in size and spacing on the white background to be reproducible as line art. Pencil work especially can approach true continuous-tone to an extent that it requires halftone screening.

Shading film. Shading film is a pressure-sensitive material on which a screen tint or other pattern is printed. The film adheres to a paper backing that is peeled away before the film is placed on the artwork. Shading film is printed in black in various patterns and in various percentages of tints. The more popular patterns include the following: conventional round-dot screen in horizontal, vertical, or diagonal directions; straight-line screens in horizontal, vertical, or diagonal directions; circular screens; diamond or square-shaped screens; and mezzotint screens. A piece of shading film that is cut larger than needed is placed over the areas of art that will appear as a shade or tone. The image is traced with a sharp knife, and the excess film tint is peeled away. The film is then covered with tissue and burnished to make it stay in that position.

Line conversion or posterization. Creating a line conversion or posterization means converting a continuous-tone photograph to line copy. This special effect is achieved by exposing a continuous-tone photograph to high-contrast line film or to the negative paper used in the diffusion transfer process without a

A three-tone posterization.

screen. The resulting negative drops out all highlight and light middletone areas and reproduces all deep middletone and shadow areas as solids. If the diffusion transfer process is used to create the line conversion, the positive image created on the receiver paper is pasted into position on the mechanical.

Original line art is seldom adhered directly to the pasteup. Instead, a paper print of the original line art is created using a graphic arts camera and diffusion transfer materials; the paper print is adhered to the pasteup. Artists often have direct access to a small graphic arts camera, which allows them to make their own diffusion transfer paper prints, or "stats." A paper print is produced by mounting the original image on the camera's copyboard, adjusting the camera for the proper reproduction percentage, mounting diffusion transfer negative paper on the film holder, making an exposure through the camera lens, and processing the photographic material. Processing is the most complicated step in making a diffusion transfer print. The exposed side

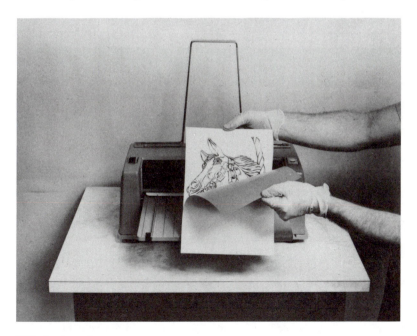

Diffusion transfer process.

of the negative paper is placed into contact with a special "receiver" paper. During processing, the unexposed areas on the negative paper are transferred to the receiver paper, creating a positive image on the receiver paper.

Continuous-Tone Art

Continuous-tone art has a range of tones from light to dark. The lightest areas are called **highlights,** the darkest are called **shadows,** and the areas in between are called **middletones.** Continuous-tone art can be in color as well as in black and white. Common examples of continuous-tone art are photographs and paintings. These all have a range of tones, from highlights to shadows, that blend smoothly into each other; there is no sharp division between light and dark. The creation of continuous-tone art—e.g., original photography—is beyond the scope of this book. However, later sections of this book discuss the methods required to convert black-and-white and color continuous-tone art into intermediate forms suitable for reproduction by printing.

Halftone made from photograph.

Unlike line art, continuous-tone art must be transformed to give the illusion of continuous tones when printed and viewed under normal conditions.

Scaling Art

In order to tell the printer what size and proportion to print the continuous-tone copy or other artwork to fit the window, the artist scales and crops the photograph by indicating reproduction size and putting fine marks in the borders. The artist also identifies the top of the photo and its location in the printed piece.

Enlargement and reduction percentages are indicated in terms of the original; for example, 50% of original (half the size), 200% of original (twice the size). Crop marks are drawn on the borders of the photograph or on a cardboard mount. Marks on a photograph or its borders should be made with a grease pencil so that they can be removed. Crop marks on a color transparency are usually scribed into the border.

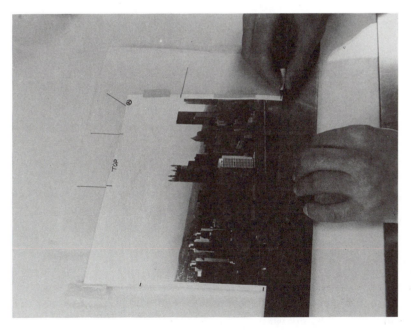

The artist is indicating the reproduction size of the photograph by using a grease pencil to place crop marks on the borders, or nonimage areas, of the photo. The artist has already identified the top of the photograph and will also write the reproduction percentage somewhere in the top border.

Reproduction Photography

After the pasteup is completed, photographic negatives or positives are made of the camera-ready copy. These films are used to make the printing plates. The continuous-tone copy is photographed separately since it may be reproduced at a different size and, more importantly, because continuous-tone copy must be photographically made into dots to be printed.

Photographic conversions can be made using contact photography or a camera. Contact photography requires the use of a **contact frame** to hold the light-sensitive material (either film or

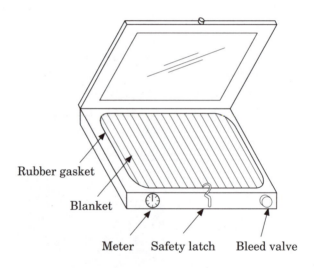

Rubber gasket

Blanket

Meter   Safety latch   Bleed valve

Glass-covered contact frame.

paper) and the copy (which must be transmission copy) together in such a way that an exposing light can be directed through the copy onto the sensitive film or paper. Contact photography can only make same-size reproductions.

To make conversions involving reflection copy or a change of size, a projection imaging system must be used. The most common of these is the **graphic arts,** or process, **camera.**

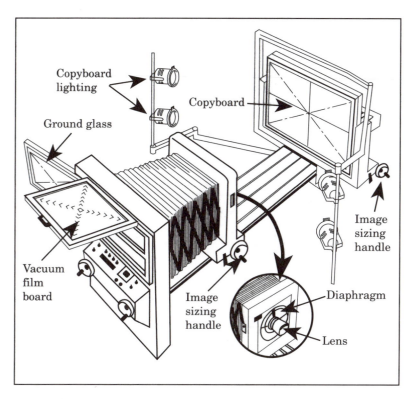

Horizontal camera.

The following are the elements of a graphic arts camera: a **lighttight "box"** or enclosure with a bellows that shields the photosensitive materials from all light except the controlled exposure light; a **vacuum film board** that holds the photosensitive material; a **lens system** of the "flat field" type—one that is used to photograph two-dimensional images; a **copy holder;** a **shutter** that can be opened to admit light from the copy through the lens into the camera; a **diaphragm,** which adjusts the lens opening to control the amount of light passing through the lens; an **exposure control unit** that determines the length of the exposure; **a means to enlarge** or **reduce the size of the image** at the film holder; and a **light system** to provide adequate and properly distributed illumination on or through the copy. The copy. The planes of the copy, the lenses, and the film holder must all be precisely parallel, and must be rigid to avoid vibration.

Such a camera is used for several purposes besides making a film image of the pasteup. Original drawings are often made larger than the size at which they are to be printed; the camera can be used to reduce them to the reproduction size (or to enlarge any that are smaller).

Photographic operations are usually performed in a darkroom under prescribed safelight conditions, with red safelighting being most common. Most graphic arts films are not affected by red light.

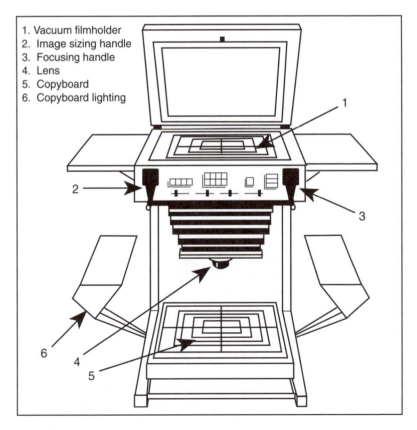

1. Vacuum filmholder
2. Image sizing handle
3. Focusing handle
4. Lens
5. Copyboard
6. Copyboard lighting

Vertical camera.

Photographing line copy. Line copy is photographed by mounting the original image on the camera's copyboard, adjusting the camera for the proper reproduction percentage, mounting high-contrast film on the film holder, making an exposure through the camera lens, and then processing the film.

After exposure, the film image must be processed—developed (made visible), fixed (made permanent), washed, and dried. Processing is generally done in one of two ways: manually, using trays of chemical solutions, and using automatic processors. The processed high-contrast film produces a photographic image that only has two tones: a clear image area and a black nonimage area. This image is called a **negative,** or **line negative,** when the original consists of type or line illustrations. Light-sensitive film consists of a photographic emulsion coated on a transparent base, such as acetate or Mylar. The emulsion contains silver halide particles. Exposure to light and subsequent processing converts the silver halide particles into black metallic silver.

Photographing continuous-tone art. Different photographic techniques are required to reproduce continuous-tone art. It has to be converted into a form that gives the appearance of a gradation of tones—an optical illusion, if you will—by a process called **halftoning.**

Continuous-tone art is photographed with a graphic arts camera through a special screen, called a **halftone screen,** that is placed in contact with the unexposed film. The halftone screen consists of thousands of tiny, closely and evenly spaced openings that are clear in the center and darken gradually toward the edges. These **vignetted** openings permit varying amounts of light to pass through, depending on the strength of the light.

As the continuous-tone original is photographed, light reflects from its surface and passes through the screen, recording the image on high-contrast film as a composite of many tiny, variously sized dots. The lighter areas of the original reflect a lot of light, which is able to penetrate enough of each vignetted opening to darken a larger area. This creates larger dots on the negative film. If the dots are large enough, they run together more or less, leaving only small areas between them that look like tiny clear dots. The shadow areas reflect very little light, which penetrates

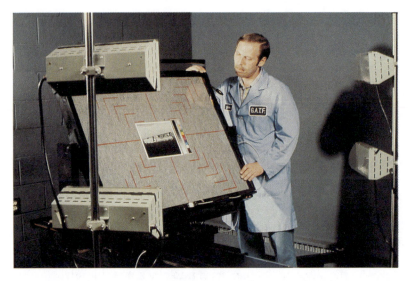

Camera operator preparing to shoot a photograph with a graphic arts camera.

only the center of the vignetted openings, resulting in very small black dots surrounded by a lot of clear space.

The halftone negative thus created has large dark dots in the picture's highlight areas and small ones in the picture's shadow areas. When made into a positive, it has small dots in the highlight areas and large ones in the shadow areas, as desired. The resulting picture thus appears to have a range of tones, yet is printable because of the clear distinction between image and non-image areas (i.e., dark dots and clear areas).

Halftone screens come in varying degrees of fineness, based on the number of lines (halftone dots) per linear inch (or linear centimeter). As a rule, the finer the screen, the greater the detail of the printed halftone. Screens used for newsprint and other rough surfaces have coarse rulings of 65–120 lines per linear inch (26–47 lines/cm). Screens used for smooth, uncoated surfaces have rulings of 120–133 lines/in. (47–52 lines/cm), and screens for glossy, coated surfaces have rulings of 133–150 lines/in. (52–59 lines/cm). Occasionally, detailed work is photographed through a very fine screen with up to 300 lines/in. (118 lines/cm); however, such detail is difficult to reproduce on press.

The most widely used halftone screens are those containing rows of round or elliptical dots. For special effects, the artist can specify screens that have concentric-circular patterns, vertical-, horizontal-, or diagonal-line patterns, random-line patterns, pebble-grain patterns, wavy-line patterns, or mezzotint patterns. These special-effect screens are typically used when detail may be sacrificed for a particular aesthetic effect.

Creating duotones. The duotone process is a special-effects technique that consists of making two halftones at different specifications from the same copy. The two halftones can either be printed in two different colors, or one in a color and the other in black, or both in black.

Duotone.

This duotone has been created using a cyan halftone and a black halftone.

Each halftone is referred to as a "printer." One is made with the contact screen at a 45° angle; the other is made with the screen at 75°. (The 30° difference is needed to avoid creating a moiré pattern. **Moiré** is an undesirable, unintended interference pattern caused by the out-of-register overlap of two or more regular patterns, such as dots or lines.)

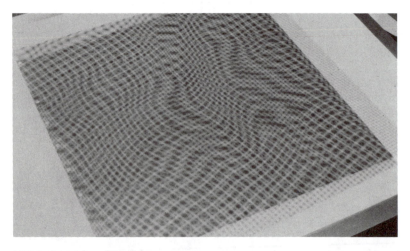

Moiré.

Most duotones are made from black-and-white reflection prints, but they can also be made from color transparencies or continuous-tone black-and-white negatives. The copy should be chosen carefully to be certain that it fits the duotone process. The photograph should have normal or slightly lower-than-normal contrast. A low-contrast print with good separation of tonal areas offers many possibilities. Photographs that have large amounts of highlight or shadow areas produce poor results.

A clear definition of the duotone technique is always difficult to give because of the numerous methods used to produce duotones. The name itself is misleading because there are more than two tones in a duotone reproduction. Alternative terms sometimes used, such as "duochrome," have their own drawbacks.

Clouding the duotone issue further is the fact that there are two schools of thought as to what a duotone is and how it is to be made. One group of printers feels that it does not matter how the negatives were made or how they are printed, as long as they present the duotone effect. An example would be to print a normal halftone on a colored paper or overprint it on a screen tint. The purist might consider these reproductions to be fake duotones. They define a "true duotone" to be two separate halftones made to different characteristics and requiring two separate impressions through the press. The following are examples of "fake duotones":

• A black halftone overprinted onto a solid color.
• A normal black halftone overprinted onto a flat screen tint of color.
• A normal halftone printed on colored paper.

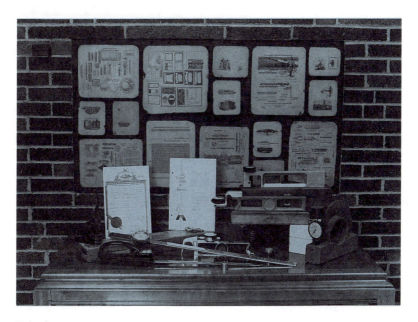

Fake duotone.

This fake duotone was made with a black halftone and a 20% cyan tint.

2 Electronic Prepress Production

Electronic prepress production is a term used to describe the process of creating documents on a computer using special software products that integrate text and graphics. Electronic prepress software enables operators to design and produce books, manuals, brochures, newsletters, annual reports, business forms, flyers, catalogs, pamphlets, posters, mailing labels, and other publications from the desktop. It is like the traditional **prepress production process** except that the images are laid out on a page *electronically*. Electronic prepress production is often called **desktop publishing (DTP)** or **WYSIWYG** (what-you-see-is-what-you-get) technology. Some of its many benefits are stated below:

• A reduction in production costs. By replacing typesetting with desktop publishing, the costs of outputting to photographic film are reduced. Most desktop publishers output directly to plain-paper laser printers, which is considerably less expensive. Also, since in-house desktop publishers control the work, they often produce it themselves instead of paying a type house to do it. If they output to film or plate, more money, as well as time, is saved. However, costs will not be significantly reduced until operators become skilled enough to use the system effectively.

• A substantial decrease in production time from writing the copy to printing the final piece. Because copy is often keyboarded using a word processing program, the text is easily imported into a page layout program where the page and design are created. Rekeyboarding, often required in traditional typesetting, is eliminated along with pasteup. Manual film image assembly and platemaking procedures may also be eliminated

• Quick verification and revision of information.

• Easier maintenance of security and supervision.

One serious drawback of desktop publishing is the tendency for one person to assume many tasks, which increases the likelihood of error in all of them. Another drawback can be a decrease in print quality depending on the system and software used.

Electronic Design

As explained in chapter one, in traditional design, the artist typically creates a series of thumbnail sketches, which are miniature drafts of a design. Graphic designers who have desktop publishing systems in house can still create thumbnails and comprehensive layouts on paper and then submit them in completed form to an electronic page layout department. The operator will carefully match all colors, type sizes, and type styles to recreate the piece on the computer by positioning each element according to the artists' layout. However, graphic designers who have access to DTP can also create and generate thumbnail concepts directly on the computer screen. Scanned photographs and line illustrations, along with the actual text in the proper typeface and font, can be imported from other software programs and integrated into the page layout template. The designer can resize type, photos, and artwork, and test different page configurations with greater flexibility. The artist may use a **graphics** or **illustration** program to create logos, manipulate type, and edit scanned images. These programs are known as either **paint** or **draw** programs. Paint programs allow the operator to alter or create images one dot or pixel at a time. The output quality of these images is dependent upon the resolution of the monitor in use. The "jaggies" or stairstep edges on curved lines are often apparent on paint images. These jaggies are less obvious when a high-resolution monitor is used.

Draw programs utilize lines to create shapes, resulting in smoother looking images. The output quality of these draw programs is dependent upon the resolution of the output device, whether it be 300, 600, 1200, or even 2400 dots per inch (dpi). Draw programs come in handy for manipulating type by rotating, skewing, stretching, or setting text to a curve. Logos, ads, and detailed graphics can be created easily on these programs. Many designers and illustrators use draw programs to design printed pieces, such as covers, posters, labels, etc. Both paint and draw files may be imported into word processing or page layout pro-

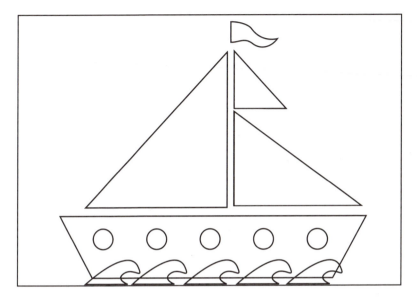

An image created using a draw program.

grams. This capability enables the artist to experiment with colors, textures, and type sizes and styles independently without incurring the expense of proofs or stats in order to create a traditional hand-drawn comprehensive. Even if the traditional design methods are used, it is important for the designer to be familiar with the features and options, as well as the limitations, of the desktop publishing system.

For design purposes, the artist may make typeface selections and place headlines and boxes (or borders) directly onto the page. The actual text or "copy" will be produced during word processing. Photographs or illustrations are often indicated by boxes or shaded areas. The designer's goal is to create a sample layout that the desktop publisher can use as a guide for the final positioning of all elements on the page. Using the computer to design facilitates experiment with the appearance, position, and size of any element on the page. It is also ideal for "visualizing" the final printed piece. Designers and their clients can preview several different concepts in near-final form much earlier in the design process.

Word Processing

During the writing process, the text for a desktop publishing job is "keyboarded" into a computer. This is done using special software known as a **word processing package.** Inputting data through a word processor is one of the most common ways to enter text into the computer. Word processing has long been used for creating letters and documents in the office environment.

Word processing applications offer many features, such as spelling and grammar checkers, search and replace functions, and formatting options. Word processing programs are still the most efficient way to enter text for letters and long documents, such as books, magazines, and newspapers.

Word processing files can be converted to work with a wide variety of equipment including traditional typesetters, personal computers, and DTP applications. Keyboarding, proofreading, and correcting can all be done efficiently on a word processor prior to the page layout steps involved in desktop publishing.

Editing is best done in the word processing program since the file should be corrected and finalized before being placed into the desktop publishing or page layout application.

Most word processing programs now provide the operator with many tools and functions that help to create quality documents in a shorter amount of time. One of the most useful features is the **spelling checker.** This utility "reads" each word in a document and checks it against an internal dictionary. If the word is misspelled or unrecognizable, the program will stop and allow the operator to correct it. The operator can also bypass the flagged entry if it is correct but not recognized by the dictionary.

Another often used utility is called **search and replace** or **find and change.** This option allows the user to globally search a document for repetitive words or symbols and make all of the changes at one time. For example, the user may need to search for an asterisk symbol (*) and replace it with a bullet (•).

Proofreading

Although electronic systems have greatly simplified prepress production, proofreading must never be overlooked. Once the word processed file has been output to paper, either the operator or a professional proofreader must proofread the copy.

Once the proof has been read and marked for corrections, it is returned to the word processing operator. Within the program, the operator makes the corrections that were indicated by the proofreader. Additional proofs may still be required, but when the text is approved, the file may be saved to disk and submitted for the page layout.

Electronic Page Layout

Printed matter is made up of two essentially different elements: (1) type matter and (2) various kinds of illustration and decoration. For printing, the characters of written language—letters, figures, and punctuation marks—must be rendered into standardized forms called **type.** The design and selection of the faces and sizes of types and their arrangement and spacing is called **typography.**

The desktop publisher uses a page layout program to define the page size, margins, and number of columns to be used on the page. These procedures are typical of the tasks involved for traditional pasteup of pages on artboards.

Next, information that will appear on every page or many pages, such as chapter titles and the title of the book, are added to the document. These are often called **running heads** or **footers.** Elements that must repeat on every page are placed on a "master page." A master page is a concept similar to the traditional overlay sheet used by pasteup artists. The computer automatically places the elements assigned to a master page into every designated page in the document.

Once the page has been "defined" as indicated by the designer's layout, the operator may begin to place the elements on the page. The text or body copy that was keyboarded in the word processor is "imported" or placed into the page layout program. When the text is in position, type sizes and styles may be assigned to the text. Headlines, captions, and other special areas of text may also be imported from a word processing file, but these are often created directly on the page by the operator. Although page layout programs generally have rather limited

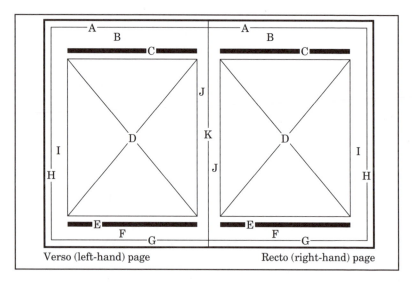

Verso (left-hand) page   Recto (right-hand) page

A layout guideline indicating: (A) head trim, (B) head margin, (C) running head, (D) type page size, (E) running foot, (F) foot margin, (G) foot trim, (H) front trim, (I) front margin, (J) back margin, and (K) fold.

drawing capabilities, most provide basic box and line tools. The **box tools** are used to border or frame ads, photos, and illustrations. **Line tools** are used to create straight or diagonal lines. Various styles, line widths, and colors can also be applied to either lines or boxes. Boxes may be "filled" with solid colors or decorative screened patterns. These drawing tools can be used to create borders and rules on the page as specified by the designer.

If the layout indicates photographs, logos, or other illustrations, the operator may save the page that has been created and use another software application and a scanner to scan images and photographs into the computer.

Scanning

Scanning is an essential part of desktop publishing since there are many functions a scanner can provide. When an image is scanned, it is said to have been "digitized" so that it can be manipulated on the computer. There are several different types

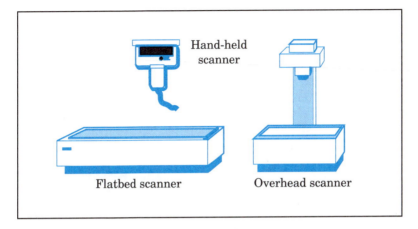

Hand-held, flatbed, and overhead scanners.

of scanners: **hand-held, flatbed,** and **overhead.** An operator uses a **hand-held scanner** by moving it across the image. Hand-held scanners are especially well-suited for scanning small items, such as logos and clip-art. They are significantly less expensive than flatbed or overhead scanners. **Flatbed scanners** are used to scan larger documents. They resemble small photocopiers. The bed is covered by a piece of glass and a flexible cover. The operator positions the image to be scanned face down on the glass of the scanner and closes the cover. Each page is scanned separately. Automatic sheet feeding attachments are also available for these types of scanners. **Overhead scanners** were designed to scan large books and/or three-dimensional objects. They resemble enlargers. The operator can place flat sheets or objects on the glass-covered copyboard or position objects on the stand.

All scanners are activated and controlled by a special software program. The operator may choose the lightness, darkness, and the reproduction size needed. Options for scanning line art and/or halftones are also available. If desired, the operator can select the type of halftone dot (round, square, or elliptical) and the screen ruling needed. The screen ruling used is often determined by the limitations of the output device. Finer screen rulings such as 133 lines/in. (lpi), 150 lpi, and 200 lpi require high-resolution imagesetters.

After positioning the image on the scanning surface, the operator often makes a **proof scan** to check the position and quality of the scan. The image's rough size and basic appearance are also shown. The original can be "cropped" so that all images on the page are not scanned. Brightness levels may also be selected to lighten or darken the picture. Once the final scan is made, special painting or editing tools can be used to clean or edit the digitized image in the computer. Each image for the job is scanned and saved to a separate file.

The ColorGetter® Prima rotating drum desktop scanner.
Courtesy Optronics, an Intergraph Division.

Color scanners are used to digitize color or black-and-white images. Color scanners are similar in appearance to black-and-white scanners. Files of color images, however, are significantly larger than those of black-and-white images.

Computer Illustration

Many times the desktop publisher will use an illustration program to create designs, logos, or illustrations directly in the computer. An operator will usually create artwork when a higher-quality graphic is required than that which can be obtained from scanning. The operator need not be artistically inclined since most computer drawing is simply combining the correct geometric shapes to create objects and illustrations. Tracing images is a common practice. A scan of the image can even be used as a template for redrawing or tracing.

These applications are often referred to as **vector-based programs.** They create images using line descriptions that appear on screen in **bezier curves.** Each line may be manipulated by moving the nodes or control points that appear on it. Illustrations created in these programs will output at the highest resolution of the printer or imagesetter because they utilize the PostScript language.

Complete color images and logos can be created in an illustration program. Any image may be resized or reshaped as required. Because the images were created on the computer, most editing or correcting is also a relatively simple process. Many times, the customer can look at the computer screen and guide the operator through the desired changes.

Bringing It All Together

After all of the scans and illustrations have been completed, the desktop publisher is ready to return to the page layout program and position these elements onto the page. This is a simple procedure. The operator locates each file from the directory and selects the appropriate command to import the file into the document. Once the graphic has been retrieved, many options may still be applied to the image. For instance, each element can be resized, cropped, lightened, darkened, or colored as required by the design directly in the page layout program.

Other adjustments may be made to the page by rearranging text, graphics, or boxes where needed. Once all of the elements are in place, the page is often output to a plain-paper laser printer to create an in-house or customer proof of the job. The client's proof may indicate changes or corrections. On the computer, the desktop publisher opens the previously created document and makes the corrections on the screen.

Upon final approval of the job, the file is generally output to a high-resolution imagesetter, which produces "typeset-quality" documents on either photographic film or paper. Photographic films and papers must be processed using special equipment and chemistry. The software program automatically produces gray scales, color bars, register marks, and crop marks on the film. If the document includes color photographs, graphics, or text, the imagesetter may also *color-separate* the file automatically. This means that the imagesetter prints each of the four process colors onto a separate film in preparation for film assembly.

Other Options

Final films produced on an imagesetter are often sent to the stripping or film assembly department for traditional film assembly. However, many electronic advancements are also being made in this area. Already, a document of several pages may be imported into another software package that will create "impositions" for the press plate. Depending on the number of pages in the document and the type of binding required, there are many different ways to imposition a job. This can be a difficult, time-consuming procedure for the stripper whereas electronic imposition systems will output the pages in the appropriate position automatically.

Impositioned pages may also be imaged directly to plate material, which saves an additional prepress step. Direct-to-plate imaging is a significant development for companies using small press formats. An even greater advancement is the ability to image the plates on the press from files generated on the desktop. When properly set up and operated, this technology enables printers to eliminate traditional pasteup, stripping, and platemaking.

DTP Job Requirements

After this brief description of desktop publishing, it may sound like a simple process that any computer operator can accomplish. It would be wonderful if this were true. However, the truth is that since desktop publishing encompasses so many functions, the desktop publisher must be knowledgeable about a number of prepress, press, and bindery procedures.

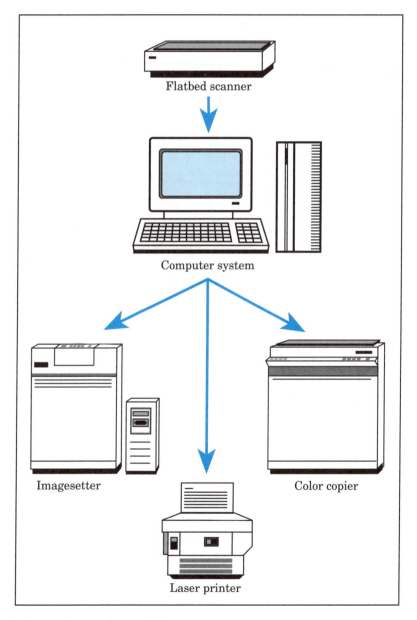

Electronic input and output devices.

DIGITAL HALFTONES

A digital halftone is merely a halftone produced by a computer system. Halftones are created to render continuous-tone images into something that can be reproduced on press. In the traditional halftoning process, photographs are reshot through a film-based contact halftone screen. The resultant image is comprised of tiny dots that can be square, round, or oval, but always evenly spaced. The sizes of the dots vary. Dots in light areas of the image are small, and dots in dark areas are larger. This varying dot size is what gives the illusion of continuous tone.

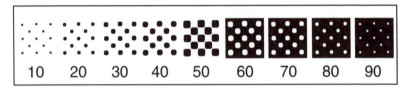

Halftone scale.

With digital halftoning, the continuous-tone photograph is converted into a digital format when it is scanned into the desktop system with a desktop scanner or video digitizer. Not just any scanner can be used. Only those with gray scale capability (the ability to recognize multiple shades of gray in the images it captures) should be used. Many scanners also have a halftone setting. This setting will produce a halftone. However, halftones produced from this setting create permanent dots, meaning that the screen angle and dot shape are set and cannot be changed. If adjustments must be made to the halftone, the image must be rescanned at a different set of values. Scanning with gray scale allows the operator a great deal of flexibility in manipulating and retouching the image without rescanning.

Several image-editing programs are designed specifically for manipulation of gray-scale images produced on a scanner. In many ways, these programs are similar to paint packages, but are geared toward images in which each dot can be one of several shades of gray.

Though image-editing programs vary widely in functionality, some features are common to all, including paint tools, selection tools, image filters, and gray-scale editing functions. Gray-scale editing functions are especially useful in improving the ultimate quality of halftones produced on the imagesetter. They typically include brightness and contrast controls. The better image-editing programs can produce photographic effects previously achieved only in a darkroom. An image can be made lighter by lowering the gray value of each pixel. It can be converted into a negative by reversing the gray values. Painting tools enable the operator to remove objects or add new ones. Cloning and texture tools allow reproduction of a portion of an image elsewhere. Selection tools enable the operator to copy an object from one image and paste it into another.

Gray Scale and Resolution

Gray scale and resolution are two important factors determining the quality of a digital halftone. Gray scale is a measure of the different levels of gray that an image can display. A continuous-tone image can show a nearly infinite number of gray values. Halftones simulate continuous tones by varying the size of halftone dots. The number of possible dot sizes determines how many shades of gray an image can show. In an image with 64 levels of gray, a dot can be any one of 64 sizes. Most current gray-scale scanners can recognize up to 256 shades of gray.

To look acceptable, a halftone needs somewhere between 64 and 256 levels of gray (plus one if you want to count white as a gray level). Images with an insufficient number of gray levels will appear to have distinct bands of gray rather than smoothly blended tones in transitional areas.

After an image is scanned, it is saved as a graphics file in one of several standard formats. TIFF, or Tagged Image File Format, is the format most widely used to save gray-scale images. It can be used with both Macintosh and PC-based software. RIFF, or Raster Image File Format, is a gray-scale file format developed for Letraset. Its major advantage is that it allows compression of gray-scale images for reduced consumption of disk space. PICT2, an extension of Apple's PICT format, can save bit-mapped images with gray-scale information. EPSF, or Encapsulated PostScript Format, is a variant of the PostScript file format that can be used to store halftone images. It does, however, consume even more disk space than uncompressed TIFF files.

Some scanner programs scan an image into the computer's memory, after which it is saved. Problems can result if the computer does not have enough memory to handle the image data. Gray-scale images (files) can be quite large, even several megabytes (MB). Other programs can scan the image directly into a disk file. Once it is saved, it may be imported into an image-editing program designed specifically for manipulation of gray-scale images produced on a scanner.

Digital halftones can be output on laser printers or high-resolution imagesetters. Like a printing press, these devices are limited by their inability to produce dots with varying intensity. However, unlike a printing press, they cannot print different size dots. To give the effect of variable-sized dots, digital output devices use a technique called **dithering**. Dithering introduces a third kind of dot called a **halftone cell.** When a dithered image is sent to a laser printer, it groups two or more printer dots into a cluster—the halftone cell—that simulates one halftone dot. To avoid confusion in referring to these different kinds of dots, printer dots are sometimes called "spots."

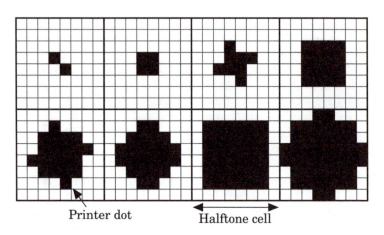

Printer dot   Halftone cell

Digital halftone dots in an 8×8 matrix, which produces 64 gray levels.

Dithering can enable the operator to get the appearance of gray scale, but with a loss in resolution, which is the density of dots or pixels on a page or display. It is usually measured in dots per inch (dpi). However, halftone resolution—also known as screen frequency—is measured in lines per inch (lpi). Halftones with high screen frequencies, or many lines per inch, have high dot densities and a sharper image. For instance, newspaper halftones have 65–100 lpi, magazine halftones generally have 120–150 lpi, and fine art reproductions are 175 lpi or higher.

STOCHASTIC SCREENING

Conventional halftones create the illusion of tones through dots of fixed spacing (screen ruling) and variable size (percent dot area). **Stochastic** or **frequency-modulated (FM) screening,** however, creates tones with variably spaced dots. *Stochastic* is a mathematical term that describes randomness. The micron spots are randomly spaced according to complex algorithms. First-order stochastic screening varies only the spacing of uniformly sized dots, while second-order stochastic screening varies both dot spacing and area. Some of the reported benefits of stochastic screening are an absence of moiré and rosette patterns.

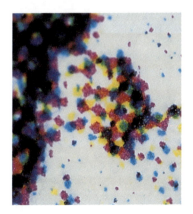 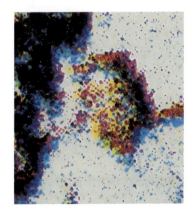

Photomicrographs of conventional 175-lpi *(left)* and stochastically screened *(right)* images enlarged 40×.

3　Color Reproduction

Much of today's printing is multicolored. The broad categories of multicolor printing are (1) **flat color** and (2) **process color.** This chapter briefly discusses flat color, but goes into detail about process-color printing, color theory, color separation, and color proofing.

A **flat color** ink is an ink specifically formulated to produce a desired hue, printed either solid or as a tint or halftone, and not designed to be mixed by superimposing on another ink or inks to produce a variety of hues. An alternative term for flat color is *spot color.* A common example of spot color printing would be a headline that is printed in a flat color or nonprocess-color ink.

An illustration can be produced in one or more colors by first designating on the artwork which areas are to be printed in solid colors and/or screen tints. A printed illustration of varied color areas using flat colors and tints is often called **fake color printing.** Depending on the number of colors printed, the illustration can approach the appearance of a full-color reproduction.

Considering the infinite range of hues that may occur in full-color illustrations, such as paintings, color photographs, and transparencies, reproducing all the hues using flat colors is impractical. Fortunately, it is possible, in theory, to reproduce any hue with just three primary colors plus black. This principle forms the basis of a full-color printing system called **process-color printing.**

Inks used in process-color printing are transparent so that they can be printed over one another to produce other hues. One opaque ink printed over another would simply block out the first one and reflect the color of the second one.

In process-color printing, each color is printed with separate printing plates. Four halftone films, negative or positive, are made of the full-color original through color filters by a process called **color separation.** The films produced record the proper densities for each of the four colors needed for the printing plates. These films are often referred to as *printers;* e.g., the magenta printer, or yellow printer.

BASIC COLOR THEORY

To understand the process of color reproduction, it is necessary to gain an appreciation of the phenomenon of color by examining the nature of light, without which color would not exist.

Light, which is a very small part of the vast electromagnetic spectrum that ranges from cosmic rays to radio waves, is a form of radiant energy that is visible to the normal human eye. Light travels in the form of waves with the color of light varying according to its wavelength. The wavelength, the distance from crest to crest of each wave, can be measured, just as the wavelengths of other forms of radiant energy on the electromagnetic spectrum are measured. The unit of measuring wavelengths of electromagnetic radiation is the **nanometer.** The length of the scale ranges from very short gamma waves emitted by radioactive material to extremely long radio waves that may be miles in length, all of which are invisible to the human eye.

Light, also called the *visible spectrum,* is a very small part of the total electromagnetic spectrum. Wavelengths of light measure from about 400 to 700 nanometers long. Although each color of light in the visible spectrum has a different wavelength, all the wavelengths together make up white light.

All the colors of the visible spectrum that form white light can be seen in a natural rainbow when rays of sunlight pass through drops of rain. The reason that the colors of the spectrum are seen as the rainbow is due to the refraction or deflection of the rays of light as they pass from one medium, air, to a denser medium, water. Because the droplets of water are more dense than air, the light rays with shorter wavelengths, such as blue, bend more as they pass through the water than the longer wavelengths of light, such as green or red.

The rainbow can also be formed by passing a narrow beam of light through a glass prism. The resultant color spectrum will appear to be divided into three broad bands of color—blue, green,

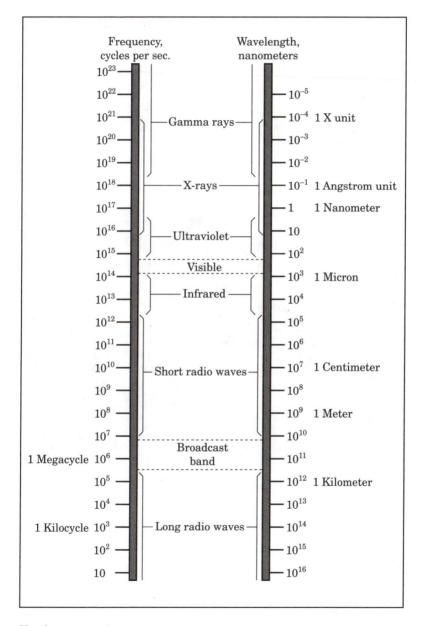

The electromagnetic spectrum.

and red—but in fact, is made up of a larger number of colors with infinitesimal variations.

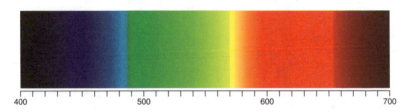

Visible spectrum.

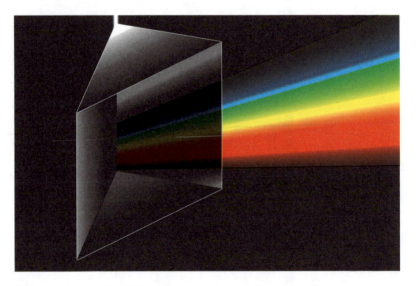

A prism splitting white light into the visible spectrum.

Additive and Subtractive Color Reproduction Processes

The colors in the spectrum are physically the purest colors possible, meaning that these colors have not been contaminated through transmission or reflection. Using a prism to split white light into its various colors, and then recombining or adding them together to form white light again, was first demonstrated and reported by Sir Isaac Newton in 1704. This is the principle of the **additive color reproduction process.** When wavelengths of colored light between 400 and 700 nm are combined in nearly equal proportions, we get the sensation of white light. When different wavelengths of light are combined in unequal proportions, we perceive new colors. The primary colors of the additive process are red, green, and blue light. In addition to these three colors, secondary colors can be created by adding any two primaries: red and green combine to give yellow; red and blue combine to give magenta; and blue and green combine to give cyan. The presence of all three colors will result in white, and the absence of all three will produce black.

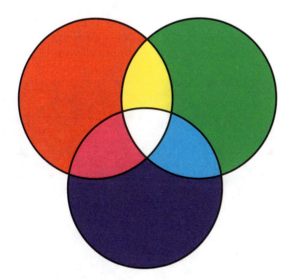

Additive color system.

Another way of demonstrating the principle of the additive color system is with three projectors and a darkened screen. Using round filters of the three primary colors, one projector projects red, another green, and the third, blue. By projecting these three colors of light, as shown, where two colors overlap, secondary colors are produced. Red and green combine to produce yellow; red and blue produce magenta; and blue and green produce cyan. Each primary color—red, green, and blue—represents one-third of the visible spectrum; therefore, yellow is made up of two-thirds of the visible spectrum, red and green. The missing color is blue. Yellow can be described as a minus blue. Magenta is also two-thirds of the visible spectrum. The missing one-third is green. Magenta is a minus green. Likewise, cyan is made up of two-thirds of the visible spectrum, blue and green; hence, cyan is a minus red. Where they all overlap in the center is white.

Note that each secondary color appears lighter than the two primary colors of each combination. Varying the intensity of any or all of the three primaries will produce a continuous shading of color. This is the principle by which color television is created. The variations of intensity can be seen by examining the red, green, and blue mosaic on the picture tube with a magnifying glass. At viewing distance, the eye does not resolve the individual colors, but mixes the red, green, and blue to form other colors.

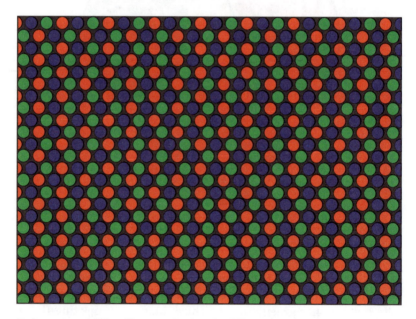

Red-, green-, and blue-filter mosaic of a color TV screen.

The three colored filters—red, green, and blue—are used in color separation to produce the films needed for making the plates to print yellow, magenta, and cyan process-color inks. To record a color on film, a filter is used to make the color appear as black or gray to the film, just as line and halftone films are made from black-and-white line copy and photographs. The red filter is used to produce the film for the cyan printer because red, which is one-third of the visible spectrum, absorbs the other two-thirds, that are shades of blue and green, making these colors appear as black or gray to the film. The green filter absorbs blue and red, to produce the film for the magenta printer, and the blue filter absorbs red and green to produce the film for the yellow printer.

The additive system starts with black, a blank TV screen for example, and adds red, green, and blue light to achieve white. By contrast, the **subtractive color reproduction system** starts with white, such as white paper illuminated by white light, and absorbs or subtracts red, green, and blue from the white paper to achieve black.

The subtraction of red, green, and blue is achieved by using transparent inks that are their opposites. To subtract red, cyan, which is made up of blue and green, i.e., minus red, is used. Green is subtracted by magenta, i.e., minus green, and blue is

Subtractive color system.

subtracted by yellow, i.e., minus blue. Yellow, magenta, and cyan are the primary colors of the subtractive color system.

Many colors can be achieved by subtracting portions of light from white paper, which reflects red, green, and blue light. For example, a combination of yellow (minus blue) and cyan (minus red) will result in green. Where all three primaries overlap, black is perceived.

Any color within the limits of the primary colors used may be obtained by varying the amount of each colorant. The subtractive color principle is used for most modern color photography and all color printing processes.

Dimensions of Color

The physical properties of color are defined in terms of hue, brightness, and saturation.

Hue. Hue refers to the name of the color. Defining a color by hue places it in its correct position in the spectrum. For example, a color said to have a "blue hue" is distinguished from yellow, red, green, etc.

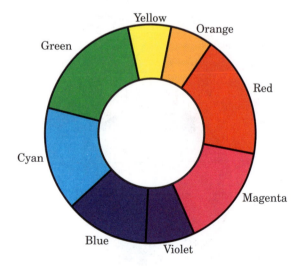

The hue component of color on an abridged color circle. The divisions on the color circle are approximate.

Brightness. Brightness, lightness, or value describes the difference in the intensity of light reflected from or transmitted by the colored image. A shirt may be described as dark blue or light blue. The hue of the shirt's color may be blue, but the terms "dark" or "light" distinguish its brightness.

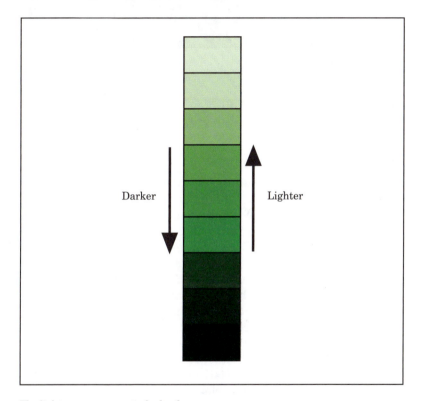

The lightness component of color for a green.

Saturation. Saturation, color purity, or color strength is the quality that describes how strongly colored something is, or how much the color differs from a neutral gray. To describe a man's tie as a dull green or a brilliant green is a distinction in saturation.

A color that is composed of only its component wavelengths is fully saturated. However, colors are usually contaminated by other wavelengths to varying degrees. For example, a gray-green

The saturation component of color for the magenta-green hue axis.

has low saturation, whereas an emerald green has higher saturation. A color gets purer or more saturated as it gets less gray.

Color Perception

Color perception depends on the object that is being viewed, the color of the light source that illuminates it, and the person who is viewing it. The object's color appearance depends on the hue or color of the pigments and dyes that are used, the purity or saturation of the color, and the color's lightness or darkness. In addition to the hue, saturation, and lightness of the pigments or dyes, the gloss of the object's surface influences the perceived lightness.

The sources of light that are used to illuminate a colored object can range from a simple incandescent light bulb to sunrays. One important characteristic of the light source is the colors that are emitted by the light itself. This can vary from the yellowish cast of the incandescent bulb, to the blue-green of a fluorescent light, to the extreme variations of natural light that occur between sunrise and sunset on clear days and overcast days.

Because the appearance of a colored object can be altered by the light source or by varying the viewing condition, a color viewing standard was necessary. In 1985, the American National Standards Institute (ANSI) specified that the color temperature of light used for viewing and evaluating colored images would be 5,000 Kelvin. Color temperature is the temperature, in Kelvin, to which a black body would have to be heated to produce a certain color radiation. As heat is applied to a black body radiator, the color changes from red to white.

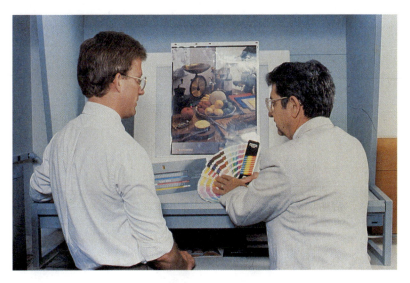

Color viewing booth.

The way in which humans perceive color is very complex and not completely understood. What is known is that very few people see color in exactly the same way. Approximately 8–10% of Caucasian males, 5% of Asian males, and 3% of African males have an inadequate perception of color. This condition was once referred to as "color blindness." The most common difficulty is accurately perceiving the red-green area of the visible spectrum. However, less than 1% of the females of all races have a color vision deficiency. The most common test for determining normal or abnormal color vision is the **Ishihara test** used by optometrists. The test consists of a series of pages that have numbers made of various size dots and colors that are dispersed over a background made up of similar dots. The ability to identify the numbers determines whether the viewer has normal color vision. Another test that is used in the printing industry is the Farnsworth-Munsell 100-Hue Test, which tests a person's ability to match colors. In this test, the viewer arranges a series of colored chips in consecutive order according to their hue. These tests are important for those involved in color reproduction, particularly as use of color continues to increase.

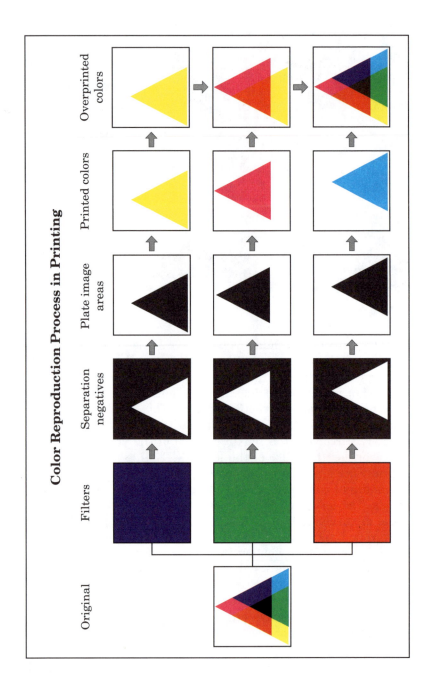

Color Reproduction Process in Printing

COLOR REPRODUCTION

Color reproduction involves many operations, starting with shooting the original photograph, and then taking it through the steps of color separation, film assembly, platemaking, and presswork. Because of the limitations of the printing process and the materials used, exact color reproduction of an original is not achievable. First, the tonal range or contrast of most originals is greater than what can be produced on a printing press with ink and paper. Second, there are no economical pure inks available, or standard white papers. Third, the color gamut, or range, of most originals is greater than that which can be produced with available inks. Knowing this, the scanner operator is concerned with tone reproduction, color correction, and gray balance in the color separations.

Tone Reproduction

Reproducing good tones is the first and foremost objective in achieving good color reproduction. The contrast range of most original photographs is generally greater than what can be reproduced by the printing process. The highlights in the original photographs are whiter and the shadows darker. Original transparencies often have a tone range greater than 3.0. For example, the highlight density, as read on a densitometer, may be 0.05, and the shadow 3.05. The range of printed reproductions rarely exceeds 2.0. Therefore, the difference in contrast must be resolved by compressing the original copy during color separation.

Color Correction

Even printing plates made from "perfect" separations will not produce the desired colors because each commercially available ink, particularly magenta and cyan, is impure and absorbs some colors that it should reflect.

Corrective measures, or **color correction,** must be taken by the color separator to compensate for the impurity of the inks that are available. Ideally, the magenta ink will absorb all of the green light portion of white light and reflect red and blue. But, it also

Marking up a proof with color correction instructions.

absorbs some blue light, which, with pure inks, would be absorbed only by yellow ink. This makes magenta ink appear as if it is contaminated with yellow ink. Since the magenta ink is not pure and cannot be ideally made, the scanner operator must compensate for this unwanted absorption in the magenta ink by reducing the size of the yellow halftone dot wherever magenta prints with yellow. Similarly, the ideal cyan ink absorbs all of the red portion of white light and reflects all of the blue and green. But, cyan also absorbs some of the blue and green light, making the ink behave as if it were contaminated with yellow and magenta inks. Therefore, wherever yellow and magenta inks are printed with cyan, the size of the yellow and magenta dots must be reduced.

Most color correction problems stem from the use of magenta inks that are too red and cyan inks that are too blue. Although yellow inks absorb principally blue, making them closest to the ideal process inks, most adjustments must be made to the yellow printer because of the blue light absorbed by the magenta and cyan inks.

In uncorrected separations, all cold colors—those with a greenish or bluish hue—become warmer or grayer, and warm colors—those that are reddish or yellowish—lack strength. Properly correcting separation negatives or positives enables printed reproductions that are close to the original.

When color separations are made on an electronic scanner, the scanner is programmed to color-correct for ink deficiencies electronically.

Gray Balance

One of the requirements of good color reproduction is that neutrals in the original photo must reproduce as neutral on the printed sheet and not show any color cast. However, equal dot areas of yellow, magenta, and cyan when printed on paper usually do not produce neutral gray. To overcome this problem, the separations have to be adjusted to each other so that neutral grays can be obtained on the printed sheet. Adjusting separations to maintain neutral gray is known as **gray balance,** another printing factor that must be controlled. Fortunately, it is not difficult to determine gray balance conditions for any combination of ink, paper, and press.

To achieve gray balance, the cyan dots must be larger than the yellow and magenta dots. Although this is a general requirement, the exact degree of imbalance varies with different ink and paper combinations. The color separator often uses a gray balance chart printed with the selected ink set and paper to determine the proper dot sizes for gray balance.

	Filters		
	B	**G**	**R**
Yellow	1.00	0.05	0.02
Magenta	0.65	1.30	0.10
Cyan	0.12	0.34	1.20
	1.77	1.69	1.32

Densities of typical process inks.

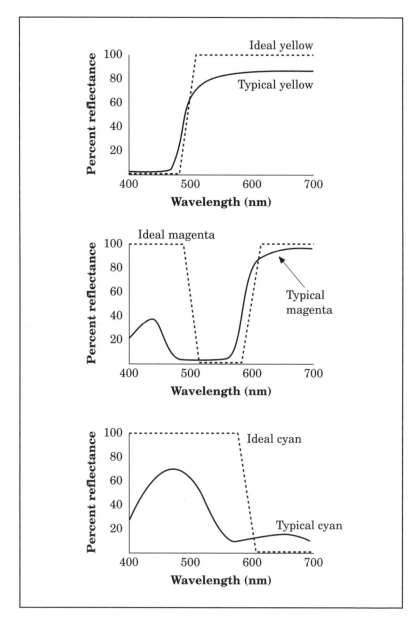

Spectrophotometric curves of typical process inks versus ideal inks.

Typically, a cyan dot area that is 10% larger than the yellow and magenta in the 30–80% region is needed to produce gray balance. This difference becomes somewhat less in the shadows and is still less in the highlights from 0–30%. Usually the yellow and magenta curves are almost identical, but it is possible to have differences between the two colors so that a little more yellow than magenta is needed to produce gray balance. Once the gray balance data is obtained, halftone positives or negatives can be made accordingly with good gray scale reproduction, provided printing and platemaking conditions remain the same.

Undercolor Removal

Undercolor removal (UCR) and its variant, **gray component replacement (GCR),** are used, in part, to compensate for some trapping and dot gain problems.

Undercolor removal is used in some color separations to reduce the size of the yellow, magenta, and cyan dots wherever black is going to print. In other words, color is removed from the neutral scale.

Undercolor removal reduces the amount of the three primary inks in the shadows and replaces them with a longer-range black printer that can carry more detail. If the 100% values of the four solid colors are reduced to 60% yellow, 60% magenta, 70% cyan, and 70% black, the total coverage amounts to 260% compared to the previous 400%. The films are described as having 260% UCR.

Gray Component Replacement

A modification of UCR is gray component replacement (GCR). Most modern scanners now have the software capable of incorporating GCR into color separations. GCR cannot be accomplished using photographic methods of color separation.

When a color is produced with a combination of cyan, magenta, and yellow, the two predominant colors determine the hue. The least dominant color darkens and gives detail to the area. For example, the color blue can be produced with the printing values of 95% cyan, 80% magenta, and 20% yellow. Since yellow absorbs the blue light, it will darken or "dirty" the color blue. In

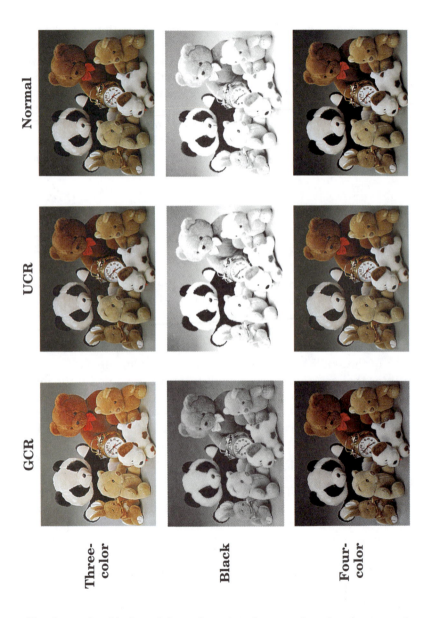

The three-color, black, and four-color prints for normal, undercolor removal (UCR), and gray component replacement (GCR) separations.

this example, cyan and magenta are referred to as the color component, and the yellow as the gray component.

The theory of gray component replacement is to take away the gray component and replace it with the appropriate value of black.

The primary advantage of GCR is that color variation on press is not as serious when GCR is used. For example, if the cyan dot in a brown color without GCR were to vary, the resulting color would shift toward either red or black. If GCR were used, and black were substituted for cyan, variations in the black dot would result in the brown getting lighter or darker but not shifting in hue. The other great advantage of GCR is the reduced use of expensive colored inks.

The major problem with GCR, like UCR, is decreased density of darker colors. For many jobs, this is not a big problem, but for others, it may be. A coverage of 300% is noticeably lighter than 400% coverage; therefore, when strong, dense blacks are required, the amount of GCR or UCR that is used would be limited. A related problem with excessive GCR is that the gloss of the reproduction will be reduced. To help correct for excessive color reduction, the process of undercolor addition is used on most scanners. With this process, it is possible to add color somewhat selectively to dark tonal areas.

In gray component replacement, the gray component may be either masked out completely or reduced to certain percentages for required printing characteristics. Many benefits can be derived from the proper use of gray component replacement. These include reduced color variation during the pressrun, lower ink costs, lower energy use for ink drying, reduced trapping and dot gain problems, and increased sharpness and contrast due to a heavier black printer.

COLOR SEPARATION

On press, each process color is printed by a separate printing unit. That means that the cyan portion of a print must be printed by one unit, which includes an inking system and a printing plate, while the magenta portion is printed by another unit, and so forth. Therefore, full-color pictures have to be separated into their component process colors and a plate made for each color.

Electronic Color Separation

Today, more than 95% of all color separations in the U.S. are made by scanners. Scanners are machines that separate color copy into its components so that it can be reproduced on a printing press. Although different manufacturers' scanners vary, all of them use the four-color principle of color separations: separating colored originals using the three additive primary colors of light in the form of blue, green, and red filters, plus a preprogrammed black printer correctly balanced with the color separations.

Scanners produce screened (halftone) printers. If scanning is done correctly, these intermediates or printers will be completely color-corrected and properly masked, and will have the right amount of undercolor removal and gray component replacement.

One important advantage of electronic color scanning is the consistency of reproduction. The scanned separations of matched originals will always match each other, provided the same information is input into the scanner for each original. These separations will match in optical density range, in the degree of color correction, and in sharpness, which means that separations can be made on the scanner uniformly day after day.

The electronic color scanner is a complicated piece of machinery that must be programmed beforehand to accommodate the kind of work done in the printing plant. It is capable of producing many special effects and can improve greatly on a poor original. Once the scanner has been programmed, operation is fairly simple and routine for standard work. However, the operator should completely understand how to use the controls in order to take full advantage of the scanner's capabilities.

Rotary-Drum Scanners

The most common type of scanner has two cylinders (or drums), one for analyzing and the other for exposing. The original, reflection copy or a transparency, is mounted on the analyzing drum and the separation film is mounted on the exposing drum. When the machine is set in operation, these two cylinders start rotating (thus the generic name "rotary drum scanner"). A scanning (or analyzing) head begins to move through the analyzing drum, pro-

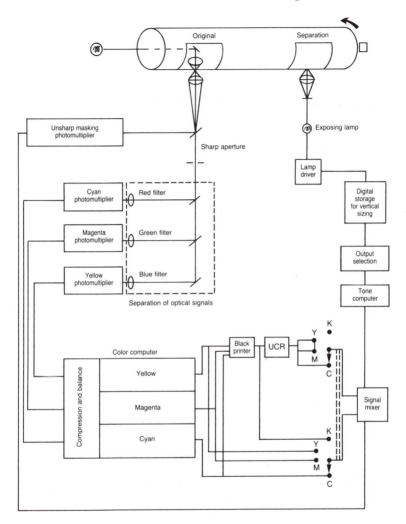

Simplified block diagram of a scanner.

jecting a tiny beam of very intense light that either passes
through the mounted copy (if it is transmission copy) or is reflected from it (if it is reflection copy). With every rotation of the
cylinder, the scanning head advances the width of a scan line
(that is, about the width of the beam of light). Although the beam
is very narrow, adjoining scans overlap slightly to produce the
effect of a continuous exposure. Depending on the scanner and

the resolution selected by the operator, these scan lines can range from 250 scans/in. (10 scans/mm) to 2,000 scans/in. (80 scans/mm).

The beam of light passes through the original and then through a small aperture into the scanner's optical system. The light passes through red, green, and blue separation filters and is focused on a photomultiplier tube that converts the optical signal into an electronic signal. The color-separated signals then undergo other modifications, such as color correction, in order to produce separations that are appropriate to press conditions and will produce the desired result. A signal for the black printer is also generated at this time.

The **color computer** in the scanner modifies the signals to suit specific inks and correct for unwanted colors. The **tone and undercolor removal computer** introduces the desired range compression, tone reproduction, and neutral gray balance and, at the same time, computes a signal for the black printer (which can be programmed to be either a full-tone black or a skeleton black).

A fourth optical signal is generated by passing light through the aperture for unsharp masking. **Unsharp masking (USM),** or **detail enhancement,** increases tonal contrast where light and dark tones come together at the edges of the images. This increase of contrast gives the reproduction increased dimensions and enhanced textures. The result is an overall increase in picture detail known as *peaking.*

Finally, the separation film is exposed. The exposing head exposes one minute portion of film at a time and advances one exposure width with every rotation of the cylinder. In addition, the time it takes to go from the scan through separation through the other modifications to exposure is so slight that both drums and heads seem to be moving in unison. The output film can be produced same-size, enlarged, or reduced, depending on the scanner. It can be either continuous-tone or halftone. And, depending on the scanner's capabilities and the output size, the separations can be produced one, two, or four at a time.

Some older rotary-drum color scanners use contact screens. Most, however, use a laser and fiber optics to generate an electronic dot pattern. Such scanners are able to electronically generate halftone patterns because separate digital computers store all the necessary information about halftone screens, rulings, and angles. Various screen rulings are available, all of which are switch-selected.

Flatbed Color Scanners

Tabletop and large flatbed color scanners are becoming more popular because of the mechanical simplicity of their design and their ability to accept rigid original copy. They are used extensively in conjunction with desktop publishing.

Typical flatbed color scanners accept transparency and reflection copy, including rigid originals. The size limits of acceptable copy vary from scanner to scanner. Some scanners accommodate originals as small as 35 mm; many accommodate originals larger than 8½×11 in. (216×279 mm). The way the original image is mounted on the flatbed color scanner also varies from model to model. On one model, the image is mounted on a small drum inserted in the front of the machine; another model has the operator mount the original copy on a special carrier, which is then put into the machine. Other models have the operator place the original directly on the flatbed.

Once the original has been mounted and inserted in the machine, the operator can preview the image on the screen of a computer. Depending on the machine and the software used in the scanner and computer, the operator can rotate the image, crop and size it, mark the highlight and shadow areas, and usually input color corrections.

The flatbed scanner uses a high-intensity quartz-halogen or pulsed-xenon fixed light source to illuminate the original. A mirror directs the light reflected from (or transmitted through) the original through a lens and then to a **charge-coupled device (CCD array)**. A CCD is a semiconductor device that is used to convert the image into electronic signals that correspond to the blue, green, and red contents of the original.

Color Electronic Prepress Systems

A **color electronic prepress system (CEPS)** is a computer-based image manipulation and page-makeup system for graphic arts applications. These systems produce, at very high speed, complete sets of separations to single- or double-page size, with all illustrations, tints, and rules in their correct locations. Some systems also integrate text.

In addition to the scanner, a traditional CEPS configuration consists of several magnetic disks capable of storing all the information needed, a computer workstation consisting of a video display terminal (VDT) with keyboard, a mouse, and sometimes a digitizing tablet.

Original transparency or flexible reflection copy is mounted on the analyzing portion of the scanner, and the scanner is programmed in the usual way for size, tone, and color correction. A high-speed scan stores all this information on the magnetic disk, instead of producing a film separation. A single job may require several originals to be scanned and stored on magnetic disks. The information stored on the magnetic disk is accessed using the keyboard and displayed on the VDT, and the job layout is placed on the digitizing table.

A freely moving mouse is used to define the relative locations of all pictures and their cropping outlines. Corners of pictures are used as coordinates, and the mouse need only be placed on two diagonally opposite corners to define a rectangular or square picture outline. In the case of irregularly shaped pictures, the mouse is moved around the outline. Using the mouse and a simple list of layout commands available on the digitizing table surface or the keyboard, the operator can define the dimensions, color, and positions of tint blocks, rules, borders, and backgrounds without needing to scan originals. All this information, in addition to the color separation data, is then stored on the magnetic disk. To produce a completely assembled page, the scanner is loaded with unexposed film and the expose button is pressed. In a single operation, the page information is called from the disk storage and is fed into the exposing head of the scanner, producing a full-page negative or positive.

The above description describes what can be termed a "traditional" CEPS configuration. These traditional systems consist of proprietary equipment from a single manufacturer. Newer systems are more modular in configuration and less of a proprietary nature. For example, routine color correction, pagination, and image assembly tasks are often handled by separate workstations and/or other electronic prepress equipment. PC and Macintosh computers, with the proper software, can now handle many of the functions that were once only possible using a high-end CEPS.

Links between desktop publishing and CEPS. Developers and users alike who have worked with high-resolution color images on desktop publishing equipment are often frustrated by the enormous file sizes and the inevitable problems associated with them, including slow display times, delays in image manipulation, network bottlenecks, inadequate RAM and disk storage, and excessively slow output times. While the results of color desktop publishing may be "good enough" for some applications, color images produced on desktop systems are nearly always of lower quality than traditional color reproduction using a high-end rotary drum scanner. CEPS users, on the other hand, have to deal with the difficulties of including type in pages assembled on their systems. It is frequently more cost-effective to incorporate the type conventionally on the stripping table, than to work with it on the system. Customers sometimes balk at the high prices associated with building pages on CEPS equipment, when some of that work could be easily accomplished on desktop publishing software.

Several systems on the market today effectively link desktop publishing and CEPS, offering users the best of each technology. These systems provide desktop publishers access to the high-resolution imaging capabilities common with CEPS, without the degradation in performance normally associated with color desktop publishing.

When using a desktop-to-CEPS link, the operator of the color electronic prepress system works from an "electronic mechanical" transferred from the desktop publishing system. The mechanical can include all type, rules, tints, and "electronic position prints" that are replaced on the CEPS by high-resolution color separations. These systems give CEPS users the ability to take advantage of PostScript text and graphics created on desktop publishing equipment. Their customers, in turn, can use the relatively low-cost desktop terminals as input devices for the much more costly CEPS equipment.

Color Proofing

A set of color separations has to be checked to make sure that the films will produce the desired result. Once the plates have been made, the press inked up, and the paper printed, it is very expensive to decide that the color balance is not acceptable. For this reason, **prepress proofs** are made for approval by the customer. They provide a way to catch mistakes, a standard to strive for when doing the actual printing, and a kind of insurance for the printer in case the customer objects to a printed product that matches the proof he or she approved.

There are two general types of photomechanical prepress proofs: **overlay proofs** and **transfer (or surprint) proofs.** An overlay proof consists of layers of transparent films, each of which is exposed in turn to one of the separations and thus carries either the yellow, magenta, cyan, or black image. These films are overlaid in register on a white base to simulate the printed images. The color images can also be viewed separately or in other combinations.

With a transfer proof, the color images are applied directly to the base material one at a time, producing a one-piece proof that resembles the printed image.

Another way of producing a color proof, called **direct digital color proofing,** does not even require a set of halftone negatives or positives. Instead, in this proofing method, digital information is used to directly image the color proofing material. Various technologies are used to image the color proofing material.

4 Film Assembly

A press typically prints several pages of a publication on each side of a press sheet. Therefore, all the photographic page images from which a printing plate, or other image carrier, is made are combined in printing position on a form called a **flat.** The flat is used to expose the plate during platemaking. Since each color printed on any side of a press sheet must have a different plate, each element to be printed in that color must have its component image in the proper place on its flat.

Assembling all of these film images (which are usually negatives in the United States) in their exact places on the flats for platemaking is often referred to as **film assembly,** or *stripping.*

The procedures used for film assembly are not so much determined by whether the film is single- or multicolor. Rather they are determined by whether the film is negative or positive.

A layout sheet must be made before the flat is started. The layout should be planned so that making the flat will be as simple as possible. It should also simplify the work to be done in the platemaking area, pressroom, and bindery. The stripper should study all instructions accompanying a job before drawing the layout. If a dummy layout or completely prepared stripping layout is furnished, dimensions must be verified. It must be determined whether the job will fit on the specified paper stock. All film images should be in agreement with the layout dimensions and fit in the designated areas.

Standard press layouts are **one-up, one-side multiple, one-side combination, sheetwise, work-and-turn,** and **work-and-tumble.** These layouts are generally classified as sheetfed layouts, but they are also used on jobs run on webfed presses. Any of the two-sided layouts can be modified to run on perfecting presses. The names of the layouts vary in different parts of the country, but the layouts are actually the same.

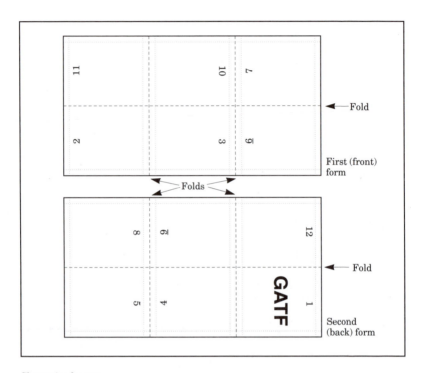

Sheetwise layout.

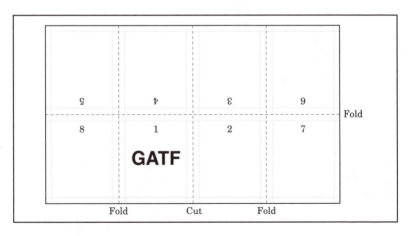

Work-and-turn layout.

Negative Film Flats

Negative film flats are prepared for the production of negative-working plates, on which the areas struck by exposing light become image areas after processing. Such a flat consists of a light-blocking paper or plastic base onto which film negatives are attached and then openings are cut. Negative line and halftone images, image control marks (e.g., trim and register marks), and quality control images may be included. Clear areas on the films transmit plate-exposure light to produce images on a negative-working plate.

The first step in assembling a negative film flat is selecting the flat material, which should be the least expensive material adequate for the job. Goldenrod paper is suitable for many single-color jobs. For multicolor jobs, orange vinyl, peelable masking film, or clear polyester with an orange vinyl or goldenrod exposure mask is required.

The layout material for a negative assembly is often the goldenrod onto which the negatives will be assembled. For book, magazine, or other production work in which the same layout will be used repeatedly, the layout may be drawn on white, coated paper or, preferably, frosted polyester. The negatives may be assembled on clear polyester, with an orange vinyl or goldenrod mask, or on peelable masking film.

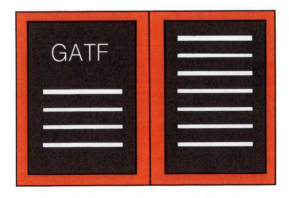

Negative film flat with film negatives mounted on an opaque carrier sheet into which openings are cut.

A sheet of layout material, somewhat larger than the size of the press plate, is placed on the layout table. The side of the layout sheet that corresponds to the gripper edge of the press sheet is aligned with a T square or the built-in straightedge of the table. If the layout sheet is to be used as the masking material, it should first be punched with the proper holes for pin register. Then it is carefully placed over register pins and taped. The film assembler draws a number of lines on the layout material to aid in positioning the film negatives. The first lines drawn indicate the plate bend and paper gripper allowances for the press on which the job will be printed. Drawn next is a horizontal line that represents the length of the press sheet. Then, horizontal and vertical centerlines for the press sheet, and trim, bleed, and other limit lines are drawn. Finally, the vertical and horizontal centerlines of each page are drawn on the layout sheet, because it is easier to position negatives to center marks than to trim marks.

The location of certain other reference lines, such as trim and fold marks, are drawn in if they do not already appear on the negatives. When the locations of halftone illustrations or other inserts are not marked by crop lines or windows on the negatives, they are drawn on the layout if there is sufficient space for all of them on a single flat. Otherwise, the marks are indicated on a complementary flat.

After the film assembler inspects the negatives for defects, each negative is trimmed slightly smaller than the space it occupies on the flat to permit taping negatives together without overlapping. Only now can the film assembler start attaching the negatives to the masking sheet. The ruled-up masking sheet is positioned wrong-reading on the stripping table, or the masking sheet is positioned over a wrong-reading layout drawn on white paper or frosted polyester. The film assembler tapes the negatives emulsion-side up to the masking sheet. Positioning marks that will be used by the press operator are added to the flat at this time.

The next step in assembling the negative film flat is to cut openings in the goldenrod/orange vinyl flats wherever printing matter or guide marks are located. If the negatives are assembled on a clear polyester carrier sheet, a masking sheet with the necessary openings is placed over the carrier sheet.

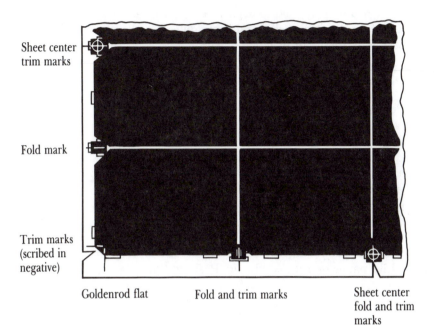

Sheet center
trim marks

Fold mark

Trim marks
(scribed in
negative)

Goldenrod flat   Fold and trim marks   Sheet center
fold and trim
marks

Trim, fold, and sheet center marks.

An exposure opening cut in the masking material around the negative to allow
light to reach the image areas in plate exposure.

Opaque is applied to negatives to block out unwanted images and to spot out pinholes and other defects. It has the consistency of a light cream for brush application.

Positive Film Flats

Positive film flats are prepared for the production of positive-working plates, on which the areas struck by exposing light become nonimage areas after processing. Such a flat consists of a clear plastic base, and the positive films are attached to it. Clear areas on the films transmit plate-exposure light to produce non-image areas on a positive-working plate.

Layouts for positive flats are made in the same way as those for negative flats. But the layout is always laterally reversed (wrong-reading) and is prepared on a separate sheet from that used for preparing the flat. The layout is prepared on coated white paper or rulable plastic. Positive films are stripped, emulsion side up, on a clear plastic sheet mounted over the layout.

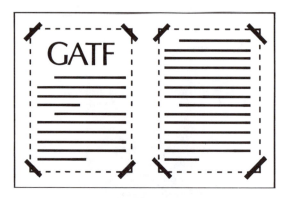

Positive film flat, with film positives mounted on a transparent base.

After the positives are inspected for general quality and retouched, or remade if necessary, they are trimmed to size. To assemble the positives, the film assembler squares up and attaches the layout to the stripping table. The clear base sheet is placed over the layout, smoothed, and carefully taped down. Register and plate location marks are transferred from the layout to the base sheet by taping positive images of the marks in position on the base sheet. The film positives are attached emulsion-side-up on this base. With positive flats, there is no masking material to remove.

Single-Color Film Assembly

In simple single-color film assembly, all the films to be assembled for one plate can go on one flat. However, if some film images would have to be assembled too close to others to permit satisfactory splicing or when one image is to be positioned in register over another on a plate, more than one flat may be made. The earlier discussion of negative and positive film assembly provides information for handling type and other line matter. The process gets more complex with halftones and other inserts. The choice among several procedures available for assembling halftones and other inserts into negative flats depends on how the artwork was prepared and on the fit between inserts and adjoining printing matter.

Attaching inserts over clear openings. Inserts, such as halftone negatives, can be attached over clear film openings if red or black masks were used on the pasteup mechanical to indicate their location. To avoid out-of-contact areas during platemaking, the tape securing the insert should be no closer to the image than ⅜ in. (10 mm). A halftone negative generally has crop marks for positioning. If these do not match exactly with the sides of the opening, the difference is usually split in positioning the film. If the halftone does not have crop marks, the film assembler positions the halftone negative by taking into account vertical and horizontal lines in the image, placement of the principal subject, and distracting edge detail that could be moved out of the window.

Complementary flats. A third method of accommodating inserts is to use two or more flats for a single color. These flats are called **complementary flats.** When a close fit between illustrations and other printing detail is necessary (and for other reasons), it is sometimes useful to put different material to be exposed to the same plate on complementary flats. Combining images on the

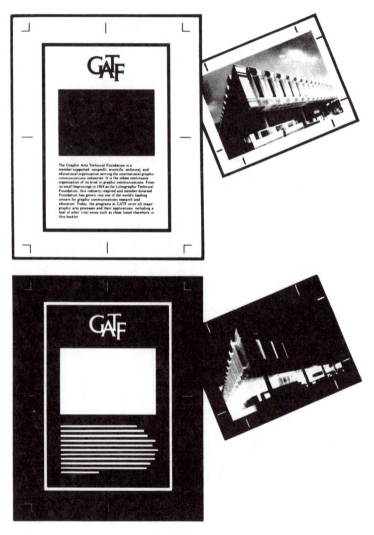

Paste-up with trim and centermarks *(top left)* and photograph with crop marks *(top right)*.

Line negative with a clear opening *(bottom left)* to receive the halftone negative *(bottom right)*.

Since windows collect dirt and scratch easily, they must be thoroughly cleaned before the halftone is attached.

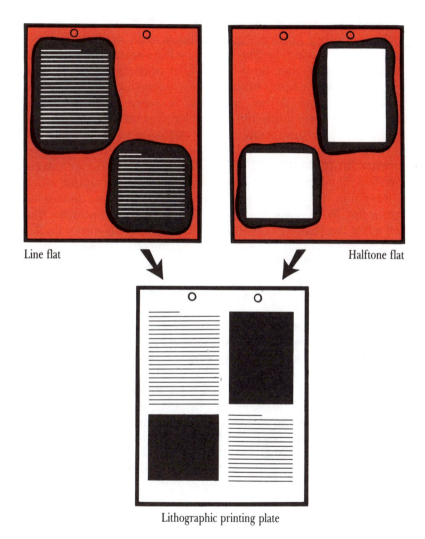

Line flat

Halftone flat

Lithographic printing plate

Example of complementary flats and how they appear when combined and exposed successively, in register, onto a sensitized surface (the lithographic printing plate).

press plate by using complementary flats is called **double printing;** if the images overprint, it is called **surprinting.**

When a screened image must touch, or butt, any other image, such as another halftone, screen tint, or rule, complementary flats must be made. The film assembler cuts openings in peelable masking film so that there is a slight overlapping of images. When only two images butt, it is easy to cut the masks with the necessary overlaps. Although several halftones, tints, and solids may butt or overlap, the film assembler may be able to plan it so that only two or three complementary flats are needed.

A line image void in a solid or tone image is called a **reverse,** or **knockout.** Making a reverse in a halftone for negative-working plates requires a suitable halftone negative and a line positive film. The two are registered to each other and assembled onto a flat. With positive-working plates, a halftone positive film and a line negative film are assembled into complementary flats.

Illustrations that fit closely to (or butt) other illustrations or text can be assembled on complementary flats and then contacted onto a single film before platemaking. This process is called **photocombining,** and the result is called a **composite negative** or **positive.**

Screen tints are screens of a single dot size used to print uniform shades in specified areas. Tints may be used with type by reversing type into a sufficiently dark tint or surprinting the type over a sufficiently light tint.

If tinted type must appear in a solid background of the same color, a screen tint is attached to a negative of the type and a positive is made from the assembly. This positive will be used as a negative when assembling the film.

Systems for image register. For high-quality film assembly, such as the use of complementary flats and multicolor film assembly, a pin register system is a necessity. The pin register system makes preplate operations more accurate and locates the image on the plate properly to minimize adjustments on press.

The stripping flat is punched with holes along its gripper edge. The hole pattern of many punches consists of a round center hole with a slotted hole on each side, thus anchoring the center and minimizing the effects of dimensional changes by dividing

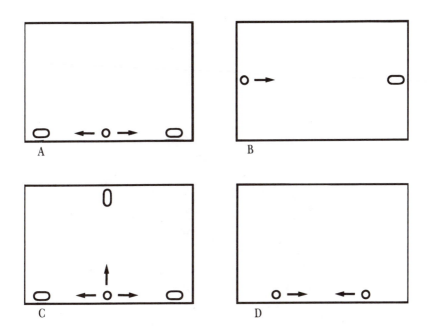

A few hole-punching patterns. Arrows indicate direction(s) of movement if film assembly material increases in size. With a flat punched like D, size expansion causes it to buckle at its center, which will result in out-of-contact areas.

them. A slotted hole is often centered near the back edge of a flat over 30 in. (762 mm).

Complementary flats are made by punching another sheet of flat material and placing it on the pins, thus avoiding the need for register marks on the complementary flat. In the plateroom, matching holes are punched into the plates. Each flat is placed on pins inserted into the plate for exposure.

Multiple Images

Multiples of a single image (for example, labels) can be produced by making a number of individual images photographically and assembling them on a flat or by contact-printing the image repeatedly onto a single composite film. Sometimes multiple images are

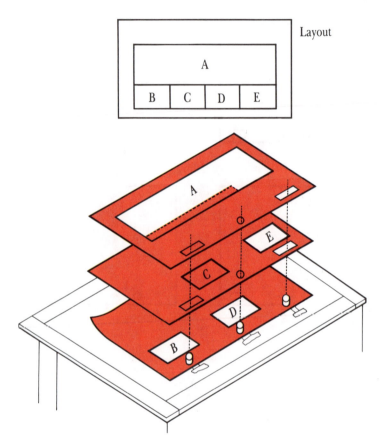

Layout

Using pin register to make complementary flats for a layout that calls for five butting halftones.

exposed to a plate from a single film image by a process called **step and repeat;** the film is repeatedly moved (stepped) and exposed by a step-and-repeat, or photocomposing, machine.

Multicolor Film Assembly

In multicolor printing, at least one flat is usually required for each printing color since each color requires its own plate. However, if the different colors are to be printed in distinctly sep-

A variety of register devices.   *Courtesy Stoesser Register Systems*

arate places, they can be placed on one flat. Each can then be exposed to its plate while the others are covered, or masked. More typically, one key-color flat (often the cyan) is assembled, and then flats of the other colors are assembled in register with it. The separation films of process-color work usually have register marks to permit exact positioning during film assembly.

Multicolor printing falls into three categories: **spot-color printing, fake-color printing,** and **process-color printing.**

Spot-color printing is adding color in selected areas. An example of spot color is having certain type blocks printed in a color other than black and having backgrounds in color, sometimes by overprinting several colors.

Fake-color printing is color printing from a black-and-white original. To make a multicolor reproduction from a line illustration, the lines of the illustration are used as outlines for the various color areas. The color and screen tint values are indicated on the original copy or on a translucent overlay sheet. The areas within each outline are stripped as small-size color panels.

Process-color printing is the production of a full variety of colors by overprinting of three standard-color inks, along with black, from a set of color-separated halftones.

Image Register

Two or more colors that are combined to produce a multicolor reproduction must have the correct positional relationship, or register, with the other colors. Two different levels of register accuracy are hairline register, the accepted standard, and loose register, where critical color register is not required: the color images are relatively independent of each other.

Another "register" term requiring definition is lap register, or **trap.** This is the overlapping of a narrow strip of one color over the other at their junction to make it easier to fit the colors together on the press. An illustration is the fitting of a line image of one color into a white space reversed into another color, and slightly overlapping the edges to avoid having any white space showing. For example, magenta type could be given a cyan background and the slight overlap would be hardly noticeable.

It is sometimes necessary to move the edge of a line image slightly outward or inward without otherwise changing the image's overall dimensions to provide trap. The image that has edges that have been moved slightly outward is called a **spread,** or "fatty"; an image with edges that have been moved slightly inward is called a **choke,** or "skinny." A spread is made photographically from a negative; a choke is made from a positive. Contact photography is used to create the spread or choke. Two common methods of producing spreads and chokes are the (1) spacer/diffusion sheeting method, in which a clear film spacer is

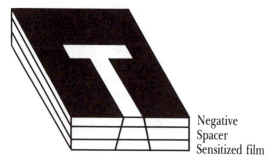

Negative
Spacer
Sensitized film

A spread made from a negative.

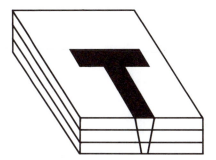

A choke made from a positive.

placed between the unexposed film and imaged film, and a sheet of light-diffusing material (e.g., translucent plastic sheeting) is placed on the outside of the contact frame and (2) the overexposure method, in which a small amount of spread or choke is obtained by overexposing a film with a matte surface.

Process-Color Film Assembly

In the assembly of process-color pages, image control marks are handled in a different way from those in single-color assembly. Layout and film positioning methods are the same, but with some additional requirements.

Rather than assembling the trim marks, center marks, and fold marks on the same flat as the line and halftone negatives, as with single-color film assembly, the marks of the four process-color flats are assembled into a single master marks flat, which also includes register marks. Alternative terms for this flat are "master flat" and "marks flat." For negative assembly of the master marks flat, the layout is ruled up on a sheet of orange vinyl with fold, center-of-sheet, and trim lines. Negative marks for trim, center, and fold are aligned with the layout lines and taped emulsion side up on the flat. Register marks are also positioned. The flat is turned over and the masking material is cut away from the marks. This flat is labeled "Master Marks." For positive assembly of the master marks flat, the layout is drawn on a separate sheet and covered with a sheet of clear polyester. Positive control marks are applied, and masking material is placed wherever images, carried by other flats, are to print.

The next step in process-color film assembly is the selection of the assembly materials. Clear polyester sheets are commonly used for the assembly of four-color separations, including negative separations. The clear material helps to locate images and place them more accurately. Since openings do not need to be cut for the images, the solid base material remains strong. For platemaking, a sheet of masking material with exposure openings is placed over the polyester. An alternative is the use of peelable masking film. It remains strong because only the membrane is cut and peeled away for exposure openings; the transparent base remains uncut, and the remaining membrane on the base provides the exposure mask.

Before the process-color images are assembled on their respective film flats, the base negative flat, which contains black-printing type, is usually assembled on orange vinyl if nothing else is to be on the flat. Clear polyester is generally used if text and black separation negatives are to be on the same flat. The type is assembled first; the separation negatives are assembled after a stripping key is developed.

The film assembler then selects one of the four process colors as the "key" color. The film flat containing that color is then assembled. All image units of the key color are fitted to the cropping masks and layout lines. They are attached to the top side of the flat material, which is pin-registered on the stripping table.

The key flat or a stripping key (a contact positive made from the key flat) is placed over the pins with a polyester sheet over the key. The negatives for the next printing color are assembled on this polyester sheet in the following manner:

The top register marks on the negative are registered using a magnifier, and the top edge is taped in place. The bottom edge is checked for register and taped. Then, the top registration is rechecked. Finally, the halftone images themselves are checked for correspondence between negative and key.

Because of the number of film flats involved in a process-color job, the film assembler must carefully label each film flat.

Before the plates are made, another proof called a **blueline** is made by putting the flats over light-sensitive paper and exposing it to intense light in a vacuum frame. The blueline is cut and folded to show how the job will look when printed. The proofreader and client then proofread the blueline against the pasteup photocopy for one final check before the job is printed. Since, it is the final opportunity to make corrections before the job is printed, it is important to make sure that everything is in place and that there are no blemishes on the blueline proof. The folded blueline is also used to check page position and proper folding.

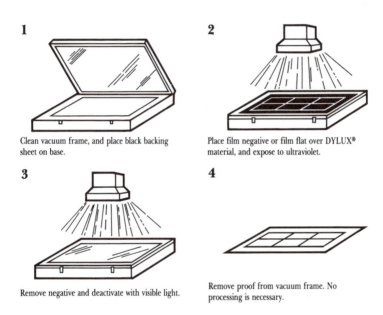

1 Clean vacuum frame, and place black backing sheet on base.

2 Place film negative or film flat over DYLUX® material, and expose to ultraviolet.

3 Remove negative and deactivate with visible light.

4 Remove proof from vacuum frame. No processing is necessary.

Production of a DYLUX® proof.   *Courtesy E. I. du Pont de Nemours & Co., Inc.*

5 Image Carriers

Creation of the image carrier is the last major prepress step in most printing processes. It is the culmination of all of the prepress functions that have come before it; generally, image carriers cannot be made to compensate for or correct flaws that have been produced in prior prepress functions without incurring considerable expense.

Plates that can be wrapped around the cylinder are by far the most common image carriers; they are used in lithography, flexography, and letterpress. Gravure printing is done primarily from mechanically engraved or chemically etched cylinders.

LITHOGRAPHIC PLATEMAKING

The lithographic plate has a base material that is either metal, paper, or plastic. The base material is coated with a light-sensitive emulsion that becomes the image area of the plate when exposed through the films prepared in the stripping area or by projection in a camera-platemaking device. An exposed and processed plate consists of two areas: the image area, which accepts ink and repels water; and the nonimage area, which accepts water and, thus, when wet, repels ink.

Most lithographic plates are imaged from a negative or positive high-contrast film flat using a **vacuum contact frame.** The vacuum printing frame holds the film flat and plate in close contact during exposure. The unit consists of two metal frames joined by a hinge; the bottom frame holds a corrugated or channeled rubber blanket with a rubber bead or gasket around its edges; the top frame contains a sheet of flawless plate glass. The bottom frame is connected to a vacuum pump by a flexible rubber tube. After the film flat and plate are placed in the contact frame, the frame is closed. The vacuum pump is turned on to remove the

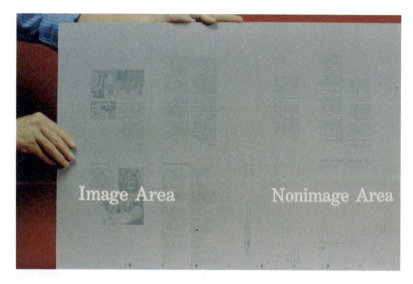

Image and nonimage areas.

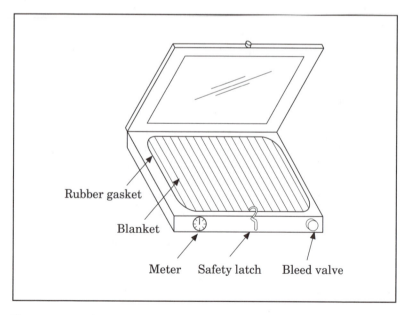

Vacuum contact frame.

air from inside the frame, causing the rubber blanket in the bottom frame to draw tightly up against the glass, squeezing the flat and plate together as the air is removed. The exposure is made using a high-intensity ultraviolet light.

Some plates are imaged using projection equipment. Others are even imaged directly from a computer database using a laser to image the plate; this method of making plates is often referred to as computer-to-plate since no photographic intermediate is used to image the plate.

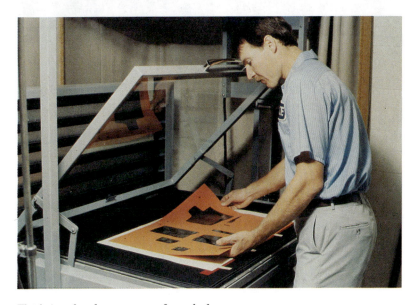

Flat being placed on a vacuum frame bed.

Several types of lithographic plates are available: surface plates, bimetal plates, photodirect plates, and electrostatic plates.

Surface plates—presensitized and wipe-on. On all surface plates, the light-sensitive coating becomes the printing image. Presensitized plates, which are coated by the manufacturer, consist of a light-sensitive emulsion, usually a diazo compound or photopolymer, that is coated on aluminum. Photopolymer coatings consist of polymers and photosensitizers that react by cross-

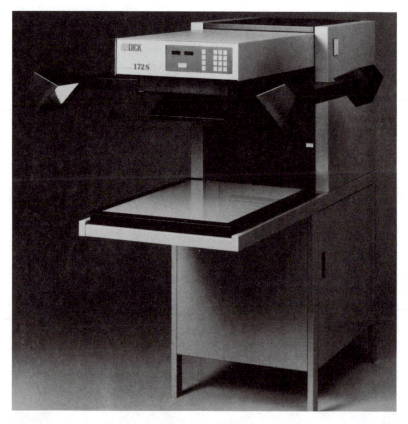

A.B. Dick model 172S platemaker.   *Courtesy A.B. Dick Co.*

linking during exposure to ultraviolet light producing a tough, long-wearing image area. Diazo coatings also react with light to produce a tough, long-wearing image area.

Wipe-on aluminum plates are chemically similar to presensitized plates but are coated with aqueous diazo coatings in the plate room using a simple roller coater.

If a lithographic plate is exposed through a film negative, it is called a **negative-working plate,** and if it is exposed through a film positive, it is called a **positive-working plate.**

Coatings used on negative-working plates are soluble in oil-based solvents or water. They become insoluble after exposure to light. A film negative of the image to be printed is placed in close contact over the coated plate, held in contact under vacuum, and then exposed for a predetermined time. The light that passes through the transparent areas of the negative polymerizes the plate coating and makes it insoluble. Where the coating is covered by the opaque parts of the negative, light is blocked and the unexposed coating remains soluble. After being exposed with light, the plate is developed by chemically removing the unexposed coating from the water-receptive nonimage areas. The exposed coating is ink-receptive and provides the printing image.

For positive-working presensitized plates, the nonimage areas are made soluble by light. Unexposed areas remain insoluble in the developer and become the printing image.

Bimetal plates. Bimetal plates, consist of two different metals, one for the image areas and the other for nonimage areas. The metals of bimetal plates are chosen so that the image metal is ink-receptive and the nonimage metal water-receptive. Bimetal plates have copper as the image metal. The nonimage metals are aluminum, chromium, or stainless steel. When copper and chromium are used together, they are usually electroplated as layers on a third metal, such as steel. Such plates are often called trimetal or multimetal plates, even though the third or base plate metal does not form the printing image.

Most bimetal plates have the image metal electroplated over the nonimage metal, such as copper on stainless steel or copper on aluminum. These plates today are presensitized as either positive- or negative-working plates. It may seem that bimetal plates are actually relief plates since one metal is above the other. The top layer of metal is so thin that its thickness is usually measured in millionths of an inch. Thus, bimetal plates are true lithographic plates.

Bimetal plates are coated and developed much like surface plates. After development, the remaining coating acts like a barrier to etching, protecting the top metal when the unexposed areas are chemically etched to expose the second metal layer.

Photodirect plates. Photodirect plates can be produced directly in either camera or projection equipment. Photodirect plates eliminate the intermediate step of making a photographic negative or positive. Because camera or projection equipment uses a lens system, the printing image can be an enlargement or reduction of the original.

If a photodirect plate is made using a camera-like platemaker, the original reflection copy (pasteup) is photographed directly onto the plate through the lens of the platemaker.

A modification of the photodirect plate is the projection plate, which is used for producing enlargements from microfilms. Projection plates are exposed and processed in specially designed projection and processing platemakers.

Electrostatic plates. Three electrostatic processes for making printing plates have been developed—**xerography, electrofax,** and **OPC** (organic photoconductors). In all three processes, an image is produced by the action of light on a photoconductive surface that has been charged by static electricity. The areas exposed to light become electrically conductive and lose their charge. Unexposed areas remain electrically charged to attract oppositely charged powder or liquid toners that become the image.

In the xerographic process, a selenium drum is the photoconductor that attracts the toners. The toners are either transferred directly, or from a rubber drum or blanket, to either paper or metal plates. The toners are then fused to the plate by heat to form the image areas.

In the electrofax process, the photoresponsive surface consists of a zinc oxide photoconductor in a resin binder that is usually coated on paper. OPC plates use organic photoconductors instead of zinc oxide. A corona produces a negative charge on the zinc oxide or OPC coating. Like selenium, the zinc oxide or OPC coating loses its charge upon exposure to light. The image is produced when a positively charged powder or liquid toner is attracted to the charged image areas. The image is then fused at high temperatures to the plate.

Electrostatic plates have been used in computer-to-plate systems in which exposures are made by computer-controlled lasers. Systems such as these are used by national newspapers using satellite transmission of complete newspaper pages.

PREPARING THE GRAVURE CYLINDER

The gravure cylinder has a copper surface that is either chemically etched or mechanically engraved to form the image. The term "intaglio" is sometimes used to refer to all printing from engraved plates (including rotogravure), but today it generally refers only to special applications such as steel die engraving. United States currency, treasury bonds and notes, and some postage stamps are printed with a copper plate or a steel die engraving. Copper plates for this type of printing may be hand-engraved, but steel plates are engraved from a hardened die.

Copper is most commonly used for gravure cylinders because it can withstand etching and engraving and maintain its integrity. It can also be easily electroplated onto the core cylinders and ground and polished to fine tolerances. For most pressruns, the copper shell is chrome-plated. After a pressrun, the copper shell is stripped or machined off, and the cylinder can be replated.

The basic method of gravure cylinder preparation with carbon tissue resist and iron chloride as an etchant did not change from the time it was introduced in 1862 until electromechanical engraving was developed in the 1960s. (Iron chloride was used to etch cylinders for textile printing as early as 1784.) For a number of years, chemical cylinder etching continued to compete with electromechanical engraving.

Currently, electronic cylinder engravers are used almost exclusively to prepare gravure cylinders. Electronic cylinder engraving is often called **electromechanical engraving** because it is accomplished on a lathe style cutting machine rather than in a chemical etching process. The copper-plated gravure cylinders are engraved with an electromagnetically controlled diamond stylus that creates the cells used in the gravure process. As many as twelve engraving heads can engrave the cylinder simultaneously, with each head producing 5,000 cells per second.

Electronic cylinder engraving equipment consists of a scanning unit, an image processor, an engraving unit, and a control center. The copy to be engraved is mounted on the scanning cylinder, which rotates in front of one or several scanning heads. The heads move horizontally across the copy as the scanning cylinder rotates. Light reflected from the copy is received by a photodiode

Electronic engraving system *(left)*; engraving cylinder with multiple heads *(right)*.
Courtesy Gravure Association of America

as analog signals. The analog signals are transformed to digital signals for use in the image processor, which performs a variety of functions. Finally, the digital information is used to drive the engraving head, which also moves horizontally in front of the cylinder to be engraved. An oscillating diamond stylus engraves as many as 5,000 cells per second in the copper-plated cylinder.

Digital filmless gravure is also growing in popularity. In this case, the job information is stored on computer disks and transferred directly to the cylinder engraving head without the generation of positive films.

IMAGE CARRIERS FOR SCREEN PRINTING

In screen printing, a woven fabric screen serves as the "printing plate." The woven fabric screen is stretched tightly on a frame, and a stencil is applied either manually or photomechanically. The stencil blocks and protects the nonimage areas of the screen, while the unblocked areas form the image. The major stencil system is **photostencil. Knife-cut stencils** are rarely used.

Knife-cut Stencils

The first knife-cut stencils were cut from paper and adhered to the underside of the screen. Most knife-cut stencils are made of film rather than paper. The two types of film used for these stencils are **lacquer** and **water-soluble.**

Both lacquer and water-soluble films are composed of two layers. The first layer, called the *backing* or *support,* is a sheet of transparent or translucent paper, vinyl, or polyester. This support is laminated to a layer of water- or lacquer-soluble coating called the **emulsion.**

The film is placed over the copy, emulsion layer up. The desired image to be reproduced is cut into the emulsion layer only. The cut emulsion is carefully peeled off, revealing the support layer. The remaining film becomes a nonimage area.

The next step in preparing the image carrier for screen printing is to adhere the knife-cut stencil to the screen. In one method of adhering the stencil, a lacquer- or water-soluble knife-cut film is attached to the stretched screen with adhering liquid. The film is placed under the screen, emulsion layer up. Lacquer or water is applied to the inside of the screen to small areas and quickly blotted dry until the entire piece of film has been covered. Adhering liquid softens the film emulsion, allowing the mesh to be pushed into it.

Another way of adhering a water-soluble film to the screen stencil is called the damp screen technique. With this method, the screen is evenly dampened with water on both sides of the prepared fabric. The stencil is placed on the wet screen, and a wet sponge is used to ensure even contact with the fabric. Finally, the excessive water is blotted away.

The area of mesh surrounding the adhered film is still open and must be blocked out or filled. This is a nonimage area and is usually blocked out with an appropriate lacquer- or water-soluble screen filler.

Photostencils

Since the mid-1950s, photostencils have been the dominant process for stencil making in the industry. Artwork for use with photostencil materials can range from simple line images to very complex combination pieces and even full-color artwork. The artwork is converted into a film positive (i.e., opaque images on a translucent or transparent support) using a graphic arts camera or a contact printing frame.

All photostencils are composed of a light-sensitive coating or emulsion that hardens when exposed to an ultraviolet light source. The photostencil material is placed in contact with the positive and exposed. The image areas of the positive absorb light. The translucent or transparent nonimage areas allow the light to pass, hardening the emulsion. When the photostencil material is processed, the image areas, which were not hardened, are washed away (developed), leaving the hardened nonimage to form the stencil. There are four types of photostencil systems: indirect, direct, capillary, and direct/indirect.

Indirect stencil systems. The indirect, or transfer, film consists of a polyester or other plastic support coated with a light-sensitive emulsion. The indirect film is placed in contact with a positive and exposed to an ultraviolet radiation source. Processing indirect film includes a short bath in a developing solution prior to washing out the unexposed image areas. The processed film is then transferred immediately to the screen. Adhering the film to the screen is accomplished by blotting the wet gel-like emulsion through the screen to remove excess moisture. The stencil, which remains on the underside of the screen, must be thoroughly dried before peeling off the support sheet. This support sheet, which held the emulsion during processing, also prevents the stencil from contracting during drying.

Direct photostencil systems. The direct stencil is a light-sensitive liquid emulsion that is coated onto the screen fabric—two coats of emulsion on the printing side and three coats on the squeegee side are commonly recommended depending on screen mesh count. Next, a film positive is placed in direct contact with the coated and dried screen, and a UV exposure is made. The unexposed areas of the stencil are washed out in warm water and allowed to dry.

The basic steps of preparing a screen printing frame using the direct photostencil system: (1) the screen is coated with a light-sensitive liquid emulsion that penetrates and fills its mesh openings, (2) the screen is dried, (3) the screen printing frame is exposed to high-intensity light that passes through a film positive, and (4) the unexposed (image) areas of the screen are washed out.

Capillary systems. A capillary system is a direct stencil film that consists of a dry liquid emulsion on a film base. The emulsion, which is coated on a support film, is placed in contact with the wet screen. By **capillary attraction,** the emulsion *rises* into the fabric; pressure is *not* used. After the screen dries, the support film is removed. The screen is then exposed with a light source, washed to remove unexposed areas, and dried.

Direct/indirect photostencil systems. The direct/indirect photostencil system is a combination of an indirect film stencil and direct emulsion. A sensitized liquid emulsion coating is squeegeed through the screen to an unsensitized piece of film underneath. This film consists of a factory-coated emulsion on a polyester, paper, or vinyl support layer that is placed in contact with the stencil side of the mesh. The liquid coating laminates the film to the screen; sensitizing is simultaneous. After drying, the support layer is peeled off. The prepared screen is then exposed and processed in the same manner as a direct photostencil.

Materials used for screens. Screens can be made from polyester, nylon, or stainless-steel mesh. Both **multifilament** and **monofilament** polyester fabric are used most often for screens.

Multifilament mesh is made up of many fine threads twisted together to form a single thread. The multifilament threads are woven together to form the screen mesh.

Monofilament fabrics are constructed of single strands of synthetic fiber woven together to form a porous mesh material. These fabrics include polyester, nylon, wire mesh, and metallized polyester. Monofilament fibers can be woven finer than multifilaments and still retain adequate open areas for easy ink passage. Wire mesh, commonly called **wire cloth,** is often used with abrasive inks, such as those used for printing on ceramics, or wherever extreme sharpness, close tolerance, and thick ink film deposits are required, as in printed circuit boards. Metallized polyester mesh is composed of a monofilament synthetic fiber, either polyester or nylon, coated by an extremely thin layer of metal.

LETTERPRESS PLATEMAKING

Letterpress printing is a relief printing process, meaning that the image is printed from a raised surface.

Although some letterpress printing is done from flat typeforms, most modern letterpress printing uses curved or flexible plates mounted on a printing cylinder. One early type of letterpress plate was the **stereotype,** which came to be widely used in newspaper printing. A pasteboard impression was made of the

Letterpress typeform.   *Courtesy Latmer & Mayer Printers & Lithographers*

typeform. Fixed inside a cylindrical form, it became the mold for a lead alloy plate. A similar, higher-quality cylindrical plate was the **electrotype.** An electrotype relief plate was made by making a hot plastic or wax mold of the typeform, electroplating the mold with a coating of copper or nickel, curving the plate into a cylinder, and making it strong and rigid with a cast backing material. An inexpensive alternative to these metal plates was the molded rubber plate. Wraparound photopolymer plates have replaced the old metal plates. Photopolymer plates are prepared from a photosensitive resin or sometimes a combination of two or more such resins. Exposing the plate to UV light through a negative polymerizes the resins' molecules and hardens the plate. The exposed resin molecules combine with each other, a process that makes these areas hard. Following exposure, the nonimage areas of the plate are washed away with an alkaline aqueous solution.

A photopolymer plate is sometimes referred to as a **first-generation plate,** since it is produced from film negatives that are created from the original. Even though a first-generation plate is defined as being created from a negative, a laser-engraved plate is one kind of first-generation plate that is not derived from a film negative. Stereotype, electrotype, and molded rubber plates are sometimes referred to as **second-generation plates** because they are made from a form, instead of a film negative.

FLEXOGRAPHIC PLATEMAKING

Flexography uses flexible raised-image printing plates and rapid-drying fluid inks. Flexo plates can be made from either natural or synthetic rubber or a flexible material called **photopolymer.** There are three basic steps in rubber platemaking: (1) making an engraving from the film negative, (2) making a mold, or matrix, from the engraving, and (3) making a rubber plate from the matrix. Photopolymer plates are made of light-sensitive polymers, or plastics. Unlike the molded rubber, photopolymer platemaking material is directly exposed to intense light through a film negative image. The exposure hardens the polymer surface. Photopolymer plates can be made from two types of materials: a precast sheet photopolymer or a liquid photopolymer.

Both rubber and photopolymer flexographic plates are flexible, and can release ink onto many different materials.

Rubber plate *(left)*, photopolymer plate *(right).*
Courtesy Matthews International Corp.

DIRECT-TO-PLATE TECHNOLOGY

Electronic publishing systems have provided a way to create metal, paper, or plastic plates from electronically assembled pages with **direct-to-plate imaging technology.** The plates from many of these systems conform to industry standards and can be used on several presses.

Going beyond the direct-to-plate product is the **direct-to-press** product. Presstek offers a printing system that combines a Heidelberg sheetfed press with direct-to-plate imaging technology. Direct-to-press technology is still being developed and fine-tuned.

Heidelberg GTO-DI that uses the Presstek direct-to-plate imaging technology. *Courtesy Presstek, Inc.*

6 Presswork

LETTERPRESS PRESSWORK

Letterpress is a method of printing in which the image, or ink-bearing, areas of the plate are in *relief*. This means that they are raised above the nonimage areas—those that do not receive ink.

Letterpress is the oldest of the major printing processes, and the only one that prints directly from type. Metal type-casting and long makeready have rendered letterpress relatively obsolete.

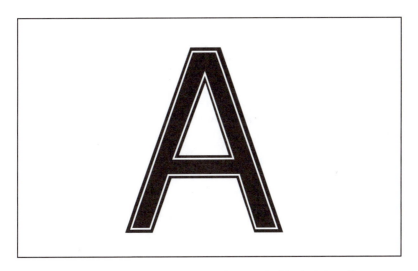

Letterpress image magnified. The image is characterized by its ink outline.

Letterpress Presses

Letterpress presses are of four basic designs: platen, flatbed, rotary, and belt. These presses print on sheets or rolls of paper depending on the application. For example, small sheetfed equipment is typically employed for short pressruns to print letterhead, envelopes, embossing, and similar products. Books, catalogs, and brochures are printed using larger equipment. Webfed letterpress equipment is appropriate for larger formats and longer pressruns.

Platen press. The platen press consists of two flat surfaces: the platen and the bed. The platen holds the paper, and the bed holds the printing form. The flat surfaces are hinged together on one side, and are opened and closed under high pressure for each printing impression. When the surfaces are open, the form is inked and a sheet is fed to the platen. The platen and bed are then closed under controlled pressure, and the sheet is printed. After printing, the press opens, the printed sheet is delivered, and an unprinted sheet is fed to the platen.

Flatbed press. The flatbed press consists of a flat bed and a rotating impression cylinder. The impression cylinder is held in a fixed position and carries the sheet as the bed containing the form passes beneath it. After each impression, the bed returns to its original position for reinking, the cylinder rises, and the press delivers the sheet. In a vertical configuration, the bed and cylinder move at the same time, and only one revolution of the impression cylinder is required for each sheet printed.

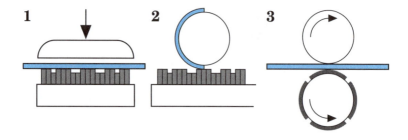

(1) Platen presses have a **flat bed** and **platen;** (2) flatbed presses also have a **flat bed,** but an **impression cylinder** instead of a *platen;* (3) rotary presses have a **plate cylinder,** instead of a *flat bed*, and an **impression cylinder.**

Rotary presses. A rotary press consists of cylindrical image carriers and impression surfaces. Both surfaces rotate in contact under pressure to transfer the image from the curved plate to the substrate. Plates are held to the cylinder by special lockup mechanisms. Plate cylinders may also be magnetic for use with steel-backed polymer plates. Paper may be sheet- or rollfed.

Multicolor press designs may consist of several printing couples (plate and impression cylinder) or several plate cylinders running in contact with a common impression cylinder. Specific ink formulations with appropriate drying characteristics are required for multicolor operations.

In webfed applications, one side of the substrate is printed at a time. The printed paper is subsequently dried and then printed on the opposite side. At the delivery of the press, the web is cut into sheets or folded into signatures for binding and finishing.

Belt press. The belt press consists of two belts to which several plates are attached. All plates for one side of the job are mounted to one belt, and all plates for the opposite side of the job are mounted to the second belt. Belt presses feed rolls of paper at approximately 1,200 ft./min. (366 m/min.). The paper is printed on one side at a time and allowed to dry after each printing. After the opposite side has been printed, the web is slit into ribbons, which are then cut into four-page signatures. The signatures are assembled (collated) into books.

LITHOGRAPHIC PRESSWORK

Offset lithography is the printing process by which a level-surfaced plate transfers an image onto an intermediate surface which transfers it onto a substrate. The image and nonimage areas of the plate are chemically separated. While offset does not mean lithography, the two words are often used interchangeably. The following are the basic steps of offset lithographic printing:

1. A plate with photochemically produced image and nonimage areas is mounted on a cylinder.

2. The plate is dampened with a mixture of chemical concentrates in a water-based solution that adheres to the nonimage areas of the plate.

3. The plate surface is contacted by inked rollers, which apply ink only to the image area of a properly dampened printing plate.

4. A right-reading inked image on the printing plate is transferred under pressure to a synthetic rubber blanket, on which it becomes reversed (wrong-reading).

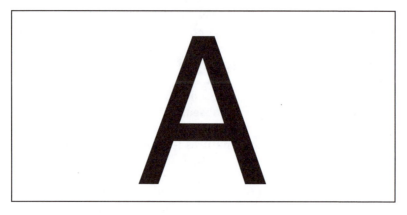

Lithographic image. Note the image's smooth edges.

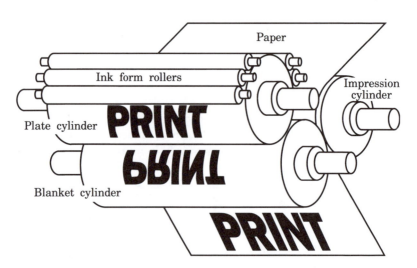

Offset lithographic printing.

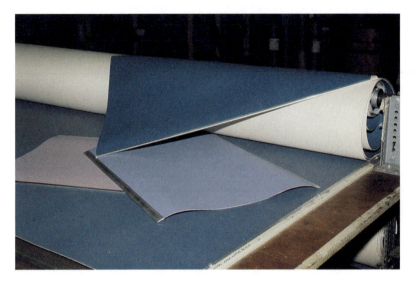

Lithographic blankets.   *Courtesy Day International, Inc. Printing Products Co.*

5. The inked image on the blanket is transferred under pressure to paper or another printing substrate, producing an impression of the inked image on the paper.

An offset lithographic press dampens and inks the printing plate and transfers the inked image to the blanket and then to the printing substrate. A sheetfed offset lithographic press feeds and prints on individual sheets of paper or another substrate. Modern sheetfed presses print 10,000–12,000 impressions per hour (iph).

A web, or web offset lithographic, press prints on a continuous web, or ribbon, of paper fed from a roll and threaded through the press. Modern web presses print more than 35,000 iph.

Most modern presses can be controlled from remote consoles from which the operator can control ink density, and adjust inking, dampening, and circumferential and lateral register.

Sheetfed Offset Lithography

A sheetfed offset lithographic press consists of a feeder, one or more printing units, transfer devices to move the paper through the press, a delivery, and various auxiliary devices (such as a con-

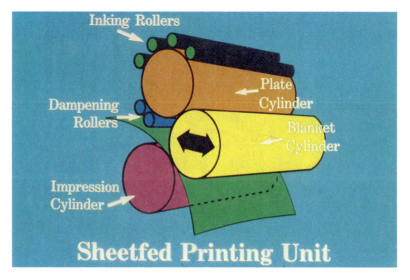

Sheetfed printing unit.

trol console). The printing unit generally includes the following:

- The **plate cylinder** carries the printing plate—a flexible image carrier with ink-receptive image areas and, when moistened with a water-based solution, ink-repellent nonimage areas.
- The **blanket cylinder** carries the offset blanket—a fabric coated with synthetic rubber that transfers the image from the printing plate to the substrate.
- The **impression cylinder** runs in contact with the blanket cylinder and transports the paper or other substrate.
- The **dampening system** is a series of rollers that dampen the printing plate with water-based dampening solution that contains additives such as acid, gum arabic, and wetting agents.
- The **inking system** is a series of rollers that apply a metered film of ink to a printing plate.

A sheetfed offset press also includes the following: a **feeder,** which lifts the sheets of paper from a pile and forwards them to the first printing unit; **transfer devices,** which facilitate sheet transport through the press (they are often auxiliary cylinders with sheet grippers); and **delivery,** which receives and stacks the printed sheet.

Sheetfed press feeder.

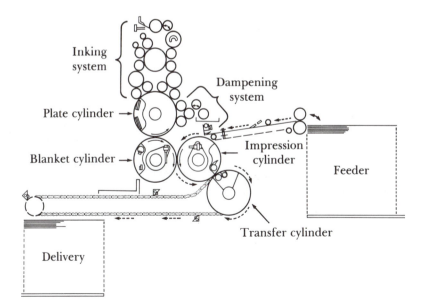

A single-color sheetfed press.

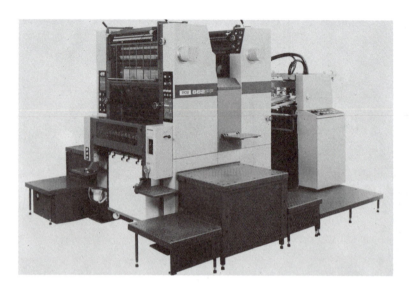

Ryobi 662 sheetfed press.
Courtesy Western Paper Co. Import Group—Ryobi

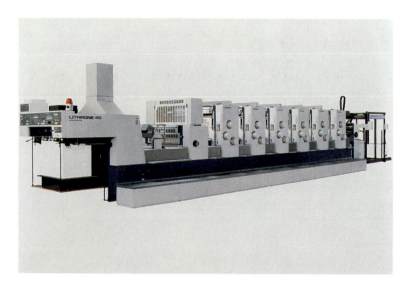

Komori Lithrone sheetfed press.
Courtesy Komori America Corp.

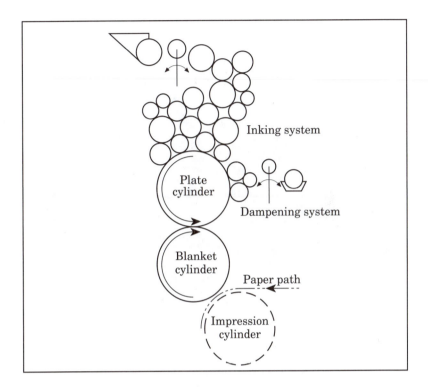

Single-color sheetfed press configuration arranged to print only one color on one side of each sheet as it passes through the press.

A variety of sheetfed offset lithographic printing presses are available. These presses can best be classified according to their offset press cylinder configurations (arrangements). Sheetfed printing unit cylinders are arranged in three basic ways:

- The single-color sheetfed press, in which there is one set of printing cylinders arranged to print only one color on one side of each sheet as it passes through the press.
- The multicolor sheetfed press, in which more than one color is printed on one side of a sheet during a single pass through the press because there is more than one printing unit.
- The perfecting sheetfed press, in which sheets are printed on both sides during one pass through the press. Various methods are used to accomplish such two-sided printing.

Web Offset Lithography

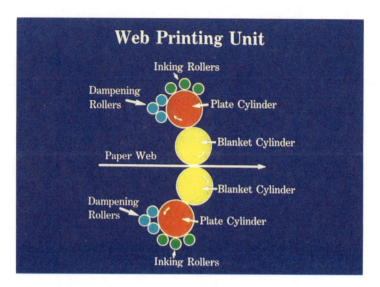

Web printing unit.

Web offset presses print on continuous webs of paper. Compared to sheetfed presses, web presses have much smaller gaps on the plate and blanket cylinders, which means that ink and water flow much more continuously. Blanket-to-blanket web offset presses lack a hard impression cylinder, which is a part of sheetfed press designs.

The web offset press consists of several sections in the following order: the **infeed,** which is where the unprinted rolls of paper are mounted; the **printing units,** which is where the substrate is printed; and the **delivery,** which is where the printed material exits the press, and is either folded, sheeted, or rewound. If the press uses heatset inks, a **hot-air dryer** and **chill rolls** will be located between the last printing unit and the delivery. The dryer removes most of the solvents from the printed ink film, and the chill rolls cool and harden the ink film.

The folder delivers folded signatures ready for mailing or for binding with other signatures to form a magazine or book.

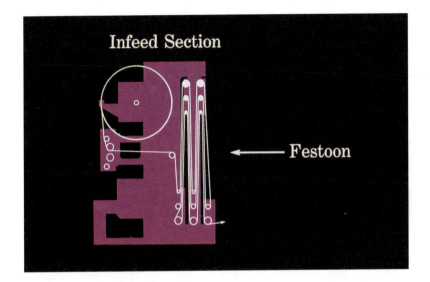

Infeed section of a web offset press.
Paper is threaded over and under many rollers, giving the impression of a web.

Web offset press hot-air dryer.
It uses high-velocity hot air to make the ink solvents evaporate from the paper.

A sheeter cuts the web and delivers flat, printed sheets. A rewinder, as the name implies, rewinds the printed web back into roll form. A folder produces signatures; a rewinder produces rolls. The bulk of web offset work involves folding and producing signatures. In-line finishing devices, such as a gluer, perforator, and diecutter may also be attached to the press delivery end.

Perfecting is the process by which a sheet or web is printed on both sides during one run through the press or unit. A blanket-to-blanket unit is therefore a perfecting unit, while a forms press may or may not be a perfecting press.

In-line describes a press with printing units that consist of an inking system, a dampening system, a plate cylinder, a blanket cylinder, and an impression cylinder. The printing units on an in-line press are *nonperfecting;* that is, they can print only one side of the web at a time.

The press consists of printing couples that are usually stacked in pairs, one on top of the other. The blanket of one couple is next to the blanket of the other couple and the web runs between them. In other words, these presses have no impression cylinders; the blanket cylinder of the top couple acts as the impression cylinder for the bottom couple, and vice versa. Therefore, a blanket-to-blanket press is perfecting.

On a blanket-to-blanket press, the printing units are usually arranged one after the other, an arrangement that offers a great deal of flexibility. With four units, one web can be run and four colors printed on each side. Or the press can be set up so that four webs are run and only one color printed per side. Anything in between is possible. For example, one web runs through the first two units, getting two colors on each side, the second web runs through the third unit, getting one color per side, and a third web runs through the fourth, also getting one color per side. This flexibility combined with high speed is what accounts for web offset's popularity.

Blanket-to-blanket press units come in two basic configurations. The most common arrangement is horizontal, in which the web runs through the printing units in a horizontal plane; the printing unit cylinders are therefore stacked vertically, one on top of the other. Vertical blanket-to-blanket presses have the web running vertically between blankets with the cylinders laid out horizontally. This arrangement allows for symmetrical printing units and provides easier access to the printing couples.

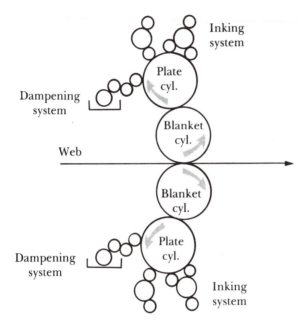

Web offset blanket-to-blanket press configuration.

Each printing unit of a common-impression-cylinder (CIC) press has one very large impression cylinder with four or five printing couples radially arranged around it. Because of the arrangement of the couples and the size of the impression cylinder, these presses are also called **satellite presses.**

A CIC press can be made to perfect in two ways. The most common means is to run the web through one unit, dry the ink, flip the web over, and run it through a second unit to print the other side. The second method prints half-webs of paper; that is, the width of the web is only half the width of the plate cylinder. The web is threaded to run along one side of the printing unit, which prints the top of it. It is then passed through a dryer and chill rolls (on a heatset press), through a turning bay where it is flipped over, and returned to the printing unit, where it runs on the other side of the cylinder. On its second pass through the printing unit, the other side of the web is printed. During operation, paper runs continuously on both sides of the press. This is called **double-ending.**

WATERLESS OFFSET PLATE TECHNOLOGY

The waterless offset plate literally means a plate that prints without any water or dampening solution. Unlike conventional lithographic offset plates, which have nonimage areas that are chemically developed to be hydrophilic, or water loving, the non-image areas of the Toray waterless plate are covered with an ink-repellent silicone rubber.

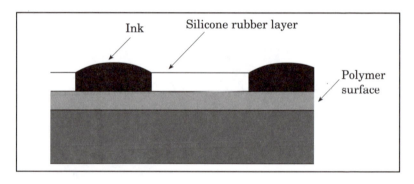

The surface of the Toray waterless plate.
Courtesy Toray Marketing & Sales (America), Inc.

The history of waterless offset technology dates back to the late 1960s when the 3M Company developed a process called **driography.** However, fraught with plate sensitivity and ink performance problems, it was never commercially available in the U.S. Ink problems may have been eliminated or alleviated if a temperature control system, which is integral to present-day waterless technology, would have been available.

Roughly a decade later in 1977, Japan-based Toray Industries introduced a presensitized positive waterless offset plate to Europe at Drupa '77. The same plate was introduced to the U.S. three years later at Print '80.

In the years since it first appeared, much progress has been made in Toray's waterless plate technology. The resulting print is said to be very sharp and capable of high screen rulings in the 200–600 lines-per-inch (lpi) range. The sharpness of the image is the result of very minimal dot gain. Dot gain is the optical increase in the size of a halftone dot during prepress operations and the mechanical increase in halftone dot size as the image is transferred from plate to blanket to paper in the lithographic offset process. In traditional offset, water emulsifies into (is picked up by) the ink. With the waterless plate, emulsification, one of the chief contributors to dot gain, does not occur.

Waterless plates cannot be developed in a conventional processor; they must be processed manually or in a special automatic processor that uses dedicated chemistries. Unprocessed plates are made of an aluminum base, followed by a primer, a light-sensitive photopolymer layer, a silicone rubber layer (this is what repels the ink in the nonimage areas), and a transparent protective film. The positive-working plate is processed by first exposing it in contact with the film flat to UV light in a vacuum frame. The light causes the silicone rubber layer to bind to the light-sensitive layer in the nonimage area. The top protective layer is then peeled off, and a developer that removes the silicone rubber layer from the light-sensitive layer in the exposed image areas is applied to the plate surface. It is said that waterless positive-working plates can achieve resolutions of 400–800 lpi.

Processing of negative-working plates begins in the same way. However, with negative film, exposure to UV light weakens the bond between the light-sensitive layer and the silicone rubber layer in the exposed image areas. After exposure, the protective cover film is peeled off and a pretreatment solution is applied. This solution strengthens the binding between the silicone rubber and light-sensitive layers in the plate's unexposed nonimage areas. The silicone rubber layer is then removed from the light-sensitive image layer in the plate's exposed areas. Negative-working waterless plates are said to achieve resolutions of 200–300 lpi. Although Toray plates are said to have the same shelf life as conventional offset plates, they are also said to be prone to scratching, perhaps even more so than conventional plates.

In order to use the waterless plate, a press must have a temperature control system to maintain a temperature at which printing is satisfactory. Two types of press temperature control systems exist: an ink oscillator (vibrator) cooling system and a plate cylinder cooling system. The ink oscillator cooling system is said to be the more effective of the two. It pumps a chilled or heated water solution (depending upon the temperature of the press) through hollow vibrator rollers on the press. Presses outfitted with the special provisions are on the market. Some are equipped with dampeners to give the printer the option of printing dry or wet. Printers can also choose to have their conventional lithographic offset presses retrofitted to use the waterless plate technology. With conventional dampening offset, a temperature control system is not necessary; the inking system is cooled by dampening solution and water.

The waterless process also uses special inks. Both the plates and the inks cost more than those used in conventional offset.

Because waterless offset technology is still emerging, American printers are cautious about embracing it. Although its environmental benefits (it does not use dampening solution, eliminating the hazards of alcohol and the headaches of substitutes), productivity advantages (quick makeready), and outstanding print quality have been touted and documented, many remain skeptical about incurring the cost to initiate and promote it. Some waterless printers have had problems with inks failing to reach a desired viscosity, resulting in ink in the nonimage areas and poor ink lay in the solid areas. Others worry about the fact that the developing solution cannot be disposed of in an ecologically safe way. Still others may be concerned about the energy needed to run the ink oscillator temperature control system.

Printers are cautioned, however, not to dismiss waterless offset as it is still under development. It remains to be seen what this technology is capable of providing once its difficulties are ironed out.

For more information on waterless offset, contact the Waterless Printing Association (WPA) in Chicago at 312/743-5677. As part of its mission, WPA strives to "educate printers about all phases of the waterless process in order to stem misinformation about it, and promote its research and development."

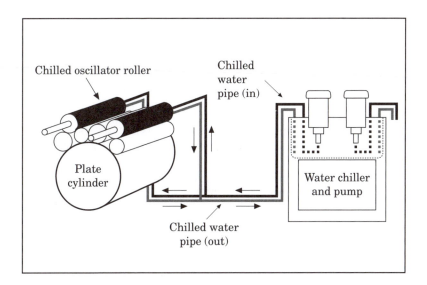

Waterless offset roller cooling system.
Courtesy Toray Marketing & Sales (America), Inc.

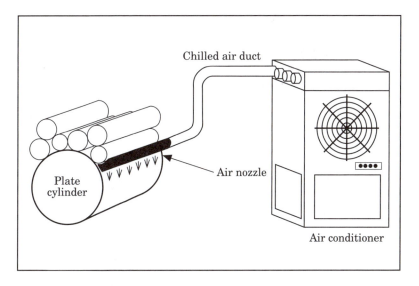

Waterless offset plate cooling system.
Courtesy Toray Marketing & Sales (America), Inc.

FLEXOGRAPHIC PRESSWORK

Most flexographic presses include four basic components: a fountain roller, an anilox (ink metering) roller, a plate cylinder, and an impression cylinder.

Fountain roller. The fountain roller (usually made of rubber) turns in an ink fountain, picks up ink, and delivers it to the anilox roller. The fountain roller and the anilox roller rotate against each other under specific pressure. The fountain roller is slower than the anilox roller, creating a wiping action that removes excess ink from the anilox roller's surface.

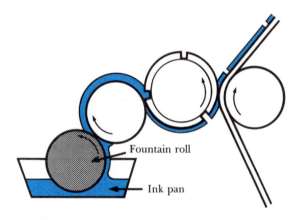

The fountain roller turning in an ink pan.

Anilox roller. The anilox roller meters, or regulates, ink flow. It is usually made of ceramic-coated steel. Its surface is engraved with small, uniform cells that carry and deposit a thin, even ink film onto the plate. The cells of the anilox roller are extremely small and can only be seen under magnification. Since the anilox roller transfers a thin, even layer of ink to the plate, the pressure and speed differential between the anilox roller and the fountain roller are considerable. These two rollers must be set to wipe excess ink from the surface of the anilox roller, leaving ink only in the engraved cells. This keyless inking system requires less energy and maintenance than keyed inking systems.

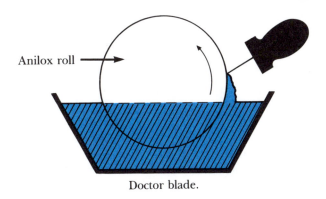

Anilox roll

Doctor blade.

An anilox roller in an ink pan with a doctor blade.

Some flexo presses use a **doctor blade** to supplement the wiping action of the fountain and anilox rollers. Others have the anilox roller rotating directly in the ink fountain. A doctor blade scrapes excess ink from the roller surface, leaving ink only in the cells of the plate.

The angle of the doctor blade opposes the direction of the anilox roller rotation and is, therefore, referred to as a reverse-angle doctor blade. It controls and evenly distributes the ink that is transferred to the plate.

Plate cylinder. The plate cylinder is a metal cylinder located between the anilox roller and the impression cylinder. The plate has raised image areas that receive ink from the anilox roller. The plate and anilox roller run against each other under light pressure; this provides for ink transfer without damaging the raised image areas of the plate.

Flexo presses accommodate several sizes of plate cylinders, which are interchangeable. In other words, an existing plate cylinder can be removed, and another one of the same or different diameter can be dropped into position.

Impression cylinder. The impression cylinder is located next to the plate cylinder. The substrate passes between the plate and impression cylinders under light pressure, which gives a kiss impression. This means that there is just enough pressure to transfer the ink from the plate to the paper.

Flexographic Press Sections

Unwind and infeed section. Flexo presses typically have four sections. Most substrates printed by flexography are fed through the press from continuous rolls, or webs. The first section of the press, therefore, is the unwind and infeed section. The speed of the unwinding substrate is regulated by braking devices. The infeed draw roll pulls the web into the press and helps to synchronize web speed and press speed, which provides register control. Proper tension control on press also helps to prevent the substrate from wrinkling, reduces slack, and reduces the chance of a web break. Flexo presses are also used to print sheeted substrates. In this case, infeed tension is not required.

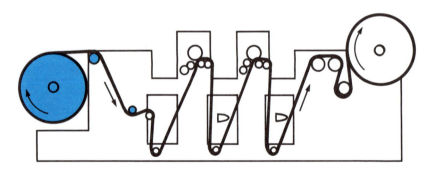

Unwind and infeed section of a flexographic press.

Printing section. From the unwind and infeed section, the paper advances to the printing section. Each printing unit on a single- or multicolor press has an inking system, a plate cylinder, and an impression cylinder. As previously discussed, the inking system consists of an ink fountain, a fountain roller, and/or an anilox roller.

Drying section. From each printing section, the substrate passes through a drying section. Dryers are placed between each color printing station and after the final printing unit before the substrate is rewound.

Outfeed and rewind section. The last section of the press is the outfeed and rewind section. This section is similar to the unwind and infeed section; however, the rewinding roll is driven to maintain tension. When rolls are rewound after printing, it is called roll-to-roll printing. Webs may also be cut lengthwise as they are rewound, producing many smaller rolls.

Substrates are not always rewound after printing. Rolls can be cut into sheets at the end of the press; some substrates (sheets and rolls) are directly fed to finishing devices that convert them into products, such as cartons, envelopes, or boxes.

Flexographic Press Designs

Flexographic presses are classified according to the arrangement of the units: (1) the stack press, (2) the common-impression press, and (3) the in-line press. Each of these can print from rolls, and all three come in varying sizes, accommodate narrow or wide substrates, and can print a variety of substrates. Flexographic presses print webs as narrow as 4 in. (101.6 mm) and less for labels, and as wide as 8 ft. (2.5 m) for products as diverse as shower curtains. Depending on the gearing of the specific press and the job to be printed, a flexo press can run at speeds as high as 2,000 linear ft./min. (609.6 m/min.).

Stack press. The stack press has all of its individual color stations arranged vertically one over another. Their configuration permits easy access, which makes on-press changes and maintenance economical. Milk cartons are often printed on stack presses because of the relative ease of changing from one carton design to another for short but varied pressruns. Some stack presses are designed to print both sides of the web during a single pass.

Common-impression press. The common-impression, or CI, press has several plate cylinders positioned around a single large

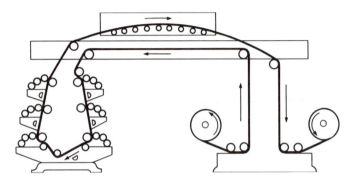

Stack press.

impression cylinder, which holds or supports the substrate. Because the press is designed with only one impression cylinder, the substrate is constantly supported from one printing station to the next. This is particularly advantageous when printing on thin, stretchable substrates, such as polyethylene film, that require reinforcement. The primary advantage of a CI press is its ability to maintain register, which is the accurate placement of one color in relation to others.

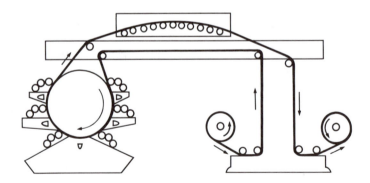

Common-impression, or CI, press.

In-line press. In-line presses contain multiple printing units that are arranged in a horizontal row, each standing on the floor. In-line presses are used for sheetfed and web production to print substrates from corrugated board to pressure-sensitive labels and newspapers. One advantage of an in-line press is that additional operations, such as diecutting, can be done following the printing stations on the press. In-line presses work well with auxiliary and converting equipment that links directly to the end of the press. Auxiliary equipment, such as web guides, web viewers, ink circulating systems, and static eliminators help to better print and handle the substrate on the press. Converting equipment performs manufacturing operations, such as slitting, bagmaking, folding, gluing, laminating, and inserting. These are in-line operations because they are executed directly in line with the press. In-line equipment can also be attached to stack and common-impression presses.

SCREEN PRINTING PRESSWORK

Equipment used for printing in the screen printing process varies from a manual-feed and squeegee operation, called a **hand table,** to a fully automatic press with mechanical feed and delivery of the substrate. Three basic screen printing systems are commonly employed: (1) the flatbed press, (2) the cylinder press, and (3) the rotary press. Most screen printing systems use a squeegee to transfer ink to the substrate.

The Flatbed Press

Flatbed presses are primarily used for printing on flat substrates of various composition, size, and thickness, ranging from very thin plastic to textiles to 1-in. (25.4-mm) board. They are either hand-operated, semiautomatic, or fully automatic.

Hand-operated screen printing tables are still used in some commercial shops. The frame is clamped into a hinge, which allows the operator to raise the screen between print strokes to remove the printed substrate and replace it with unprinted substrate. The speed and quality of the hand table operation have been improved. Vacuum tables or beds, which keep the substrate stationary during printing, improve print quality and multicolor registration. Counterweights and larger handles are attached to the squeegee to increase printing speed and maintain a constant angle between the screen and the squeegee. Hand tables are often found alongside highly developed automated presses. They can be used for test runs of packages that will eventually be mass-produced either with automatic screen printing presses or another printing process.

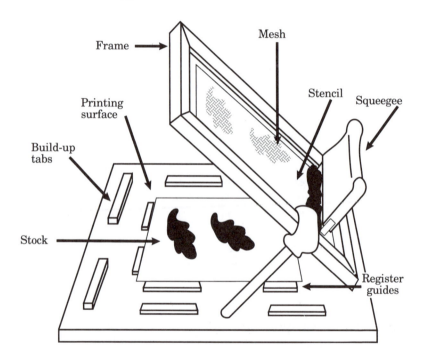

Screen printing process.

Semiautomatic flatbed presses work on the same principle as hand tables except the squeegee and frame lift are mechanized. The squeegee's consistent stroke pressure and blade angle improve production and print quality. Vacuum beds are used to keep substrates in position during printing. Some semiautomatic flatbed presses employ manual feed and delivery, while others have manual feed but automatic delivery.

The **automatic flatbed press** and the **automatic cylinder press** are two press designs used by most screen printers. An automatic flatbed press can print on flexible and rigid substrates—as thin as paper or as thick as 0.75-in. (18-mm) Masonite. During the printing cycle of an automatic flatbed press the sheet-like substrate is automatically fed and registered on a stationary vacuum flatbed. The screen is held in a carriage, which brings it into printing position above the sheet. Image transfer takes place as the mechanically controlled squeegee moves across the screen. After the impression is made, the carriage moves away from the bed and the squeegee returns to its starting position, coating the screen with a layer of ink called the **flood coat.** This is accomplished by a metal blade attached to the back of the squeegee that contacts the screen after the impression stroke. The flood coat returns ink to the starting position and deposits a thick layer atop the screen but does not force it through the image areas. The excessive ink prevents the image

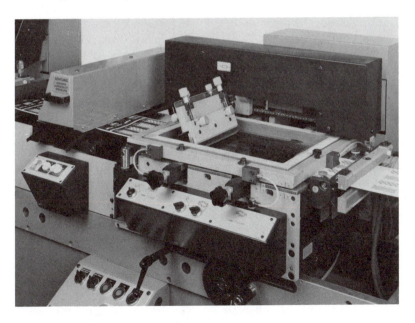

Automatic flatbed screen printing press printing on a continuous roll of paper.
Courtesy Screen Printing Association International Technical Services

areas from drying between printing strokes. Most automatic presses use the flood coating method. After the printed substrate is mechanically removed, the press repeats the printing cycle.

Press sizes vary, ranging from an 8½×11-in. (215×279-mm) format to a 60×69-in. (1.5×1.8-m) format. Larger presses can be specially ordered. Speeds range from over 2,000 impressions per hour (iph) on smaller presses to over 1,000 iph on larger ones.

There are many variations of the flatbed principle, some of which are used in printing T-shirts, textiles, wallpaper, and electronic circuits.

Whether the press has manual feed and delivery, or automated devices in any combination, the basic flatbed principle exists for all variations.

The Cylinder Press

The basic parts of the automatic cylinder press consist of a screen carriage, a squeegee, and an impression cylinder. During the printing cycle, the impression cylinder, which is carrying the substrate, and the screen carriage both move, but the squeegee remains stationary. The cylinder has grippers at the leading edge, which clamp the substrate as it is fed in. The substrate is held firmly to the cylinder's surface by vacuum. As the cylinder and substrate turn toward the delivery end, the screen slides toward the feeding end of the press, causing the fixed squeegee to force ink through the image areas. At the end of the printing stroke, the substrate is removed and delivered, and the screen slides toward the rear of the press in position for the next cycle.

Cylinder presses with automatic feed and delivery systems operate at speeds of up to 4,000–6,000 iph. Sheeted substrates are commonly handled on these presses.

A stationary squeegee is mounted in a sliding screen, which moves simultaneously over the revolving substrate. The substrate takes the place of the impression cylinder. Presses that print irregularly shaped objects can be fully automatic, semiautomatic, or manually operated. Printing speed is dictated by the size and shape of the substrate and the printing equipment used.

The container press is used in printing a wide variety of round, oval, or tapered substrates, such as bottles, pails, dials,

Cylinder screen printing press.   *Courtesy Stork X-cel, Inc.*

sports equipment, and toys. There are few limitations when screen printing irregularly shaped objects. They range in size from 50-gallon drums to small lipstick containers. In some instances, flexible plastic bottles are inflated to stabilize the printing surface. Tapered substrates, such as bottles, are printed from screens with good elasticity and specially shaped squeegees that conform to the surface.

The Rotary Press

A rotary press consists of a nickel-plated, round-hole, cylindrical screen that contains a squeegee-like blade inside the cylinder. The screen rotates over a continuous roll of paper or fabric. Its mesh is coated with a photosensitive emulsion and exposed in contact with a film positive. The screen is then processed by methods similar to most photostencil materials.

On the rotary press, the squeegee remains stationary and forces ink through the rotating screen as a continuous roll of substrate passes beneath it. Ink is continuously pumped inside to maintain high printing speeds. The web, which varies from lightweight gift wrap to thin paperboard to a continuous roll of light-

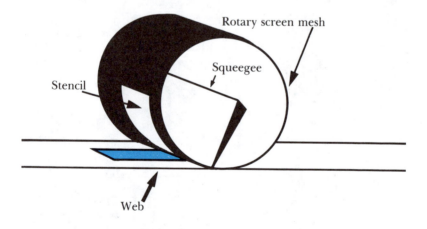

Basic principles of a rotary screen printing press.

weight fabric, may be fed through the press at speeds of up to 200 ft./min. (61 m/min.). On multicolor presses, each unit has its own screen, which is used to apply a designated color or a clear final coating. At the end of the printing cycle, the web is transferred to slitting and sheeting units. The slitter splits the sheet vertically; subsequently, the sheeter horizontally cuts the split web into sheets.

GRAVURE PRESSWORK

The intaglio, or recessed, images on the gravure cylinder and the special ink-handling mechanism that transfers the ink to the cylinder and then to the substrate distinguish a gravure press from presses used for the other printing processes. During gravure printing, the cylinder is immersed partially in ink, its surface is wiped clean by the doctor blade, and the ink remaining in the recessed cells of the image carrier transfers to the substrate as it passes between the impression roller and the printing cylinder on each unit.

Sheetfed and rotogravure printing presses have the same basic components. Each printing unit on the gravure press consists of a printing cylinder that carries the etched or engraved image; an ink fountain that applies ink to the cylinder; a doctor blade that wipes the excess ink from the cylinder; an impression cylinder that forces the substrate against the printing cylinder; and a system of rollers that feeds the substrate between the impression and printing cylinders.

Sheetfed Gravure Presses

Sheetfed gravure presses are used for printing short-run jobs: particular kinds of packaging, fine art reproductions, and some postage stamps and specialty products. They are also sometimes used as proof presses, although rollfed proof presses are preferred for higher accuracy in gravure publications printing.

In sheetfed gravure printing, grippers move the sheets from the feeder stack through the printing units and dryers to the delivery where the sheets are restacked. There are several sheetfed gravure press configurations. A simple, single-color unit or a multicolor press, which can print on both sides of the sheet simultaneously, may be used, depending on the job requirements. However, because of the high cost of gravure plate and cylinder preparation, gravure sheetfed presses are not very competitive with sheetfed offset presses and, thus, are less common.

Rotogravure Presses

Most gravure presses used today are rollfed rotogravure presses. The substrate is fed through the press from a roll in the unwind section. The roll of substrate is placed on the gear-driven unwind shaft. It is then fed, or webbed, through a series of rollers designed to control the tension of the substrate as it runs through the press. The dancer roller, an important roller in this series, is driven by a regulator, which moves up and down, continually changing the tension of the web in reaction to what is happening elsewhere in the web roll. The web travels through the printing units and dryers and is either rewound in the delivery or sent to an in-line finishing unit. The rewind unit is similar in configuration, but the order of the components is reversed. When the web

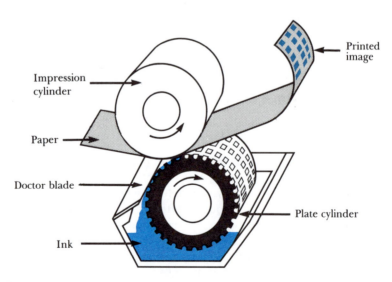

Rotogravure printing.

exits the last printing unit, it moves through another series of rollers, including another dancer roller, before it is taken up on the rewind shaft, or led to the finishing or folder unit.

On older presses, the tension of the web is governed by mechanical and pneumatic forces. The dancer roller in the unwind unit is connected to a brake control arm that is attached to an air regulator valve. In the rewind section, the dancer roller is weight-loaded, rather than air-loaded. Tension is further governed in the infeed unit by a pneumatically controlled nip roller and a geared drive roller.

Cerutti rotogravure press.   *Courtesy North American Cerutti Corp.*

Another system has been designed for precise control of web tension on newer presses. The motors in the unwind and rewind units have been designed to react within microseconds to tension signals from the dancer rollers. The dynamics of both dancer rollers are different. They are virtually weightless pendulums that send signals through microprocessors to the unwinding and rewinding motors. The motors respond equally to either increase or decrease tension. This sophisticated monitoring method allows the press to print a variety of substrates at high speeds.

As the web moves from one printing and dryer unit to another, it winds around various rollers, called **carrier,** or **idler** rollers, which help to maintain proper tension.

The path of the web is variable. Its exact path is determined in part by press design and the substrate run. If fewer colors are needed, some printing units are bypassed when the press is webbed. In publications work, the web is usually rerun or "backtracked" for double-sided printing and drying. For packaging, printing on one side is often the norm.

It is also possible to splice two webs together while the press is running at full speed by using automatic splicing devices, which are sometimes called **flying pasters.** Automatic splicing devices are very useful because the run length of a job often exceeds the length of a single web.

Ink Fountain

The ink fountain is actually one part of a more complex inking system. In one inking system, the ink is stored in a tank and pumped into an applicator that sprays it on the entire printing cylinder. The fountain does not act as a reservoir in this system, instead it serves as a collecting pan that holds the excess ink sprayed by the applicator and removed by the doctor blade. The excess ink is returned to the ink tank for reuse. Such recirculation also helps to keep the ink pigment in suspension and permits viscosity control. In another inking system, the printing cylinder is coated with ink either by being immersed in the ink fountain or by coming in contact with an intermediate inking roller that has picked up ink from the fountain. Still other gravure inking systems combine immersion and spraying.

Maintaining ink viscosity throughout the pressrun is very important. Several instruments can be incorporated in the ink fountain to measure viscosity and automatically add the necessary amount of solvent.

Doctor Blades

The doctor blade consists of a main blade and a backer blade. Its base material, thickness, and the angle at which it is mounted are determined by the variables of press design, the ink to be used, and the chosen substrate.

Doctor blades are usually made from spring steel. Other materials that may be used include stainless steel, plastic, and, to a lesser extent, brass, bronze, and rubber. The point at which the doctor blade is adjusted to fit depends on the diameter of the printing cylinder. The angle at which it operates can range from steep to almost flat.

Whenever a modification is made anywhere on a printing unit, the wiping action of the doctor blade must be checked to ensure that proper ink coverage is maintained. If the doctor blade is not angled properly, too much ink may remain in, or be removed from, the recessed cells on the printing cylinder. Properly angled blades will also last longer.

Press Rollers

The impression roller on a rotogravure press is a rubber or composition roller that is positioned over the printing cylinder. Rubber, neoprene, and Buna N are among the materials used to make gravure press impression rollers.

The backup and rider rollers minimize deflection, or bowing, of the impression cylinder. The backup roller is located above the impression cylinder, and the rider rollers are located above the backup roller.

7 Nonimpact Printing

Nonimpact printing is simply the creation of images without the image carrier impacting the substrate. Electrophotography (xerography, electrofax, and laser printing), ink jet, magnetography, electrography or ionography, and thermal transfer are among the nonimpact processes currently in use.

ELECTROPHOTOGRAPHY

Electrophotography is based on the technology of early office photocopiers. In those systems, dry or liquid toner formed an image directly on paper that was coated with a photoconductive layer. In the copier, this layer was electrically charged, exposed to the original document through an optics system, developed with toner in the image areas, and finally fused, usually with heat.

Electrophotography departs from these early copier systems in two important respects. The first is the indirect transfer concept. The second departure from conventional office copiers is the use of a laser to produce a latent image on the intermediate image carrier. Image files received directly from computers provide the bit stream to drive the laser.

The electrophotographic process works in the following way: First, an aluminum drum that has been coated with a selenium alloy photoconductor is passed under a series of corona wires in the dark to get a uniform charge. Lenses and mirrors light the copy and reflect it to the photoconductor where a latent or electrical image is produced on the photoconductor. The light that reflects from the white nonimage area of the original copy dissipates the charge in this area on the photoconductor. Since the black image does not reflect light, the charge on the photoconductor is maintained in the form of the copy image. Toner particles carrying an opposite charge are then applied to the surface of the

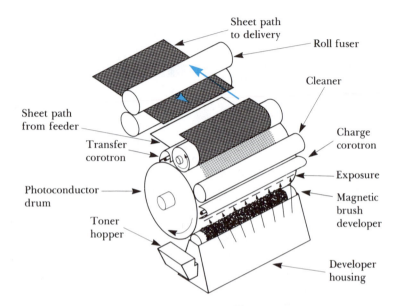

The electrophotographic process.

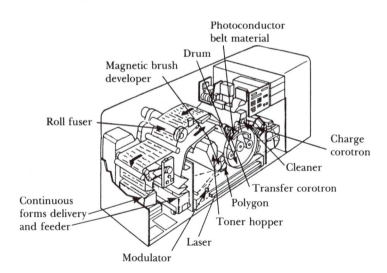

Electrophotographic laser printer for continuous forms.
Courtesy International Business Machines Corp.

Courtesy Xerox Corporation

DocuTech Production Publisher.

photoconductor drum by a magnetic brush or cascade system. The magnetic brush system mixes the toner with a carrier, usually in the form of iron filings, and carries it to the drum. This results in the toner particles transfusing to the drum and adhering to the image area by electrostatic attraction. In a cascade system, toner particles are poured, or cascaded, over the drum. The toner is attracted to the charged image areas.

When the toner image is brought into contact with a sheet of paper, a strong charge is applied to the back of the sheet, transferring the toner image to the paper. The image is bonded to the paper by heat, pressure, or both.

INK JET PRINTING

The basic requirement for creating an image with ink jet systems is to generate a controlled stream of individual droplets. Secondly, the forming of the character on the printing medium requires either controlling the droplets in their path to the printing medium—their trajectory—or turning the droplet stream on and off as the source of the ink jet stream, the "nozzle," moves along the printing medium.

The way that the image element is placed on the printing medium is basically the same in all ink jet systems. In ink jet printing, ink jet droplets are placed only where the image requires it. The background areas are left unmarked, either because the droplets are intercepted before they reach the printing substrate or because no droplets are generated in the first place.

All ink jet systems are compatible with a bit stream of digital image information. An ink droplet is essentially akin to a bit in a data stream. Therefore, droplet formation and control, while differing greatly from one ink jet process to another, always takes place in response to high-frequency digital electronic signals.

Continuous Ink Jet

Early ink jet systems employ a continuous stream of ink droplets producing pixels in the appropriate vertical location on the printing medium while the print head itself moves horizontally. The

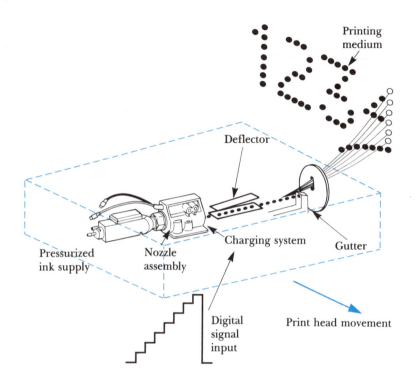

Digital continuous ink jet.

combined effect causes characters to be printed along a line or band of the printing medium. The three basic elements in such continuous ink jet systems are the **nozzle,** the **charging system,** and the **deflector.** Liquid ink under controlled pressure enters the rear of the nozzle as shown. The liquid stream is divided into a series of individual droplets through the pulsating contractions and expansions of a ceramic element in the ink passage. These pulsations result from acoustic or piezoelectric action, an effect through which certain materials respond mechanically to the application of high-frequency electric excitation applied to their surface. The frequency of droplet formation is usually a hundred or more kilocycles per second.

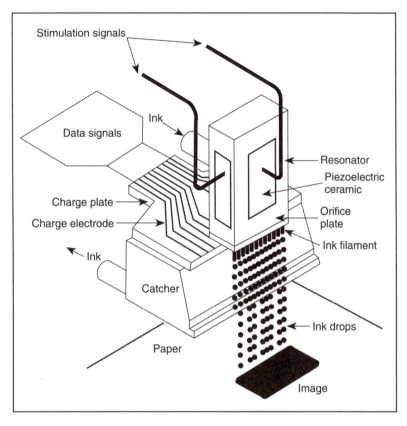

Single-row, high-resolution ink-jet printhead.   *Courtesy Eastman Kodak Co.*

Electrostatic forces are used to control the trajectory of the ink droplets from the nozzle exit to the printing medium. Pulses of electric voltage—the input to the system—place charges at the desired level on each ink droplet. The charge level induced on each droplet represents the desired target position of the droplet in the image being created. During subsequent passage between a pair of deflector plates, kept at a predetermined fixed voltage, each droplet is moved vertically by an electrostatic force corresponding to the charge it carries. Droplets with no charge are not deflected and are intercepted by a barrier or "gutter," from where they are recirculated to the ink reservoir. The complete assembly producing this ink droplet stream moves horizontally in the device and thus forms characters on the printing medium. The ink is formulated to adhere to the substrate and to dry quickly, thus forming the final printed image.

The need for better image resolution, higher productivity, and greater design simplicity has led to the development of binary continuous systems. These systems also use the principle of piezoelectric droplet generation in the nozzle. Ink flows through a piezoelectric crystal sleeve. High-frequency contractions cause the stream to be divided into droplets. It is a binary system in that the charge level that the image input signal induces on the ink droplets at the nozzle exit is either on or off. The droplets move in one of two paths. In accordance with the binary image input signal, the deflector diverts the charged droplets toward the printing medium, while uncharged droplets move straight to the gutter for recirculation.

Drop-on-Demand Ink Jet

Another general category of ink jet printers is called **drop-on-demand,** or **DOD.** With one DOD design based on the piezoelectric effect, the nozzle consists of a cylindrical element surrounding the jet stream; contractions of this element cause the droplets to be formed. In this application, however, the crystal movement is caused directly by the digital image signal, and drops are generated intermittently in accordance with that signal. To produce an image, the drum carrying the substrate revolves and the print head moves along the drum axis.

In an alternate design of a piezoelectric drop-on-demand system, a pulsating piezoelectric crystal is placed at the rear of the nozzle. Intermittent movements of this crystal cause drops to be expelled from the nozzle whenever an image element is to be printed. The air chamber surrounding the nozzle exit improves the rate and control of droplet generation. Again, to produce an image, the drum carrying the substrate revolves and the print head moves along the drum axis.

With a thermal ink jet, ink droplets are created by the application of localized short and precisely timed pulses of heat energy. This DOD process is also known as *bubble jet*. The print head for this system consists of several capillary channels, each with a small electrical resistor embedded in the channel wall. Heat generated when pulses of electricity pass through this resistor produces local ink evaporation and the formation of a bubble. The resulting pressure pulse causes a droplet to be ejected, after which the bubble collapses and returns the ink in the capillary to its normal liquid state. In an array of such channels, droplet ejection controlled by a binary image signal stream causes an image to be formed, as in the other DOD systems discussed.

8 Binding and Finishing

The bindery is often the location of all production procedures that are performed after presswork. Besides binding, **finishing operations,** such as folding, trimming, diecutting, foil stamping, and embossing, are also performed in the bindery. Finishing is also work done in line with the press but subsequent to actual presswork. Binding and finishing must be considered from the very beginning of a job, even if the job is to be bound and finished outside of the printing plant. If a printing job is not well planned, it may not be suited to the available equipment, resulting in loss of time, money, or even the entire job.

The **imposition layout,** which is a diagram indicating the positioning of pages to be printed on a sheet, is an important planning tool. It is used to determine how a sheet should be folded. A variety of imposition manuals are available from binderies and folder manufacturers.

This chapter covers the methods and equipment used for cutting, folding, assembling, binding, trimming, and, finally, finishing printed material. The binding method used is the key to the associated operations.

PAPER CUTTING

Paper may be cut before printing to ensure square sheets and before collating, folding, diecutting, or shipping if the images are printed in multiples, such as with work-and-turn or work-and-tumble impositions. The most common cutter is the guillotine, or straight cutter, which is available in many sizes and models, from small, operator-powered cutters to large, computer-controlled models, which all share several common features: a knife, a bed or table, side guides, a back gauge, and a clamp. The knife, which is bolted to a knife bar, is mounted near the front of

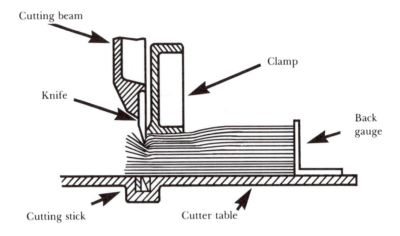

Principal parts of a guillotine paper cutter.

the cutter. The bed is a flat metal table where the paper is placed for cutting.

Sheet positioning, which is important for accurate squaring and cutting, is achieved with a side guide and a back gauge. The

Automatic spacer paper cutter.   *Courtesy Consolidated International Corp.*
This paper cutter is equipped with air cushion tables, split back gauge, and an interchangeable cassette memory system.

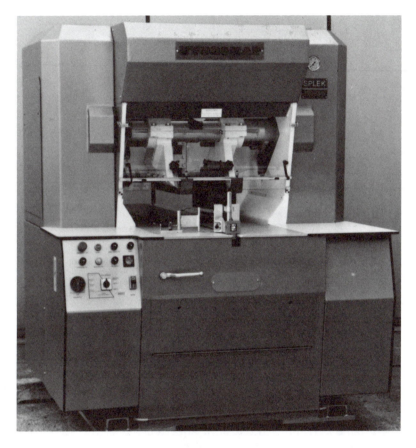

Hydromat three-knife hydraulic trimmer.   *Courtesy Vijuk Equipment, Inc.*
This trimmer operates at up to 25 cutting strokes per minute.

side gauges, which are perpendicular to the knife, are stationary, but the back gauge can be moved to accommodate various cutoff lengths.

The clamp is a metal bar that is positioned parallel to and slightly behind the knife. It compresses the pile of paper and holds it in place during cutting.

A cutting layout must be prepared before sheets are cut. It indicates the position of cuts, the sequence, final size, and any other pertinent information. The paper to be cut is placed on a stock table, press skid, or an automatic lift near the cutter for easy access. The spacing of the cutter back gauge is set for the first cut, or for the whole sequence when cutters have automatic spacing. The first lift is winded and jogged to avoid sticking and to align press sheet guide edges. The lift is stacked against the cutter's side guide and back gauge, then the clamp and knife are activated and the sheets are cut.

Automatic spacing may be controlled by magnetic tape, but the modern high-speed guillotine cutters have microcomputer-controlled spacing. Some even have memory to store programs for later use. These cutters are designed for high-speed, high-volume production cutting, and in most binderies, they include auxiliary devices, such as pile lifts, automatic loaders and unloaders, sheet joggers, conveyor lines, and vacuum waste chutes.

Guillotine cutters must have built-in safety features, such as two "on" buttons, a nonrepeating knife, safety bolts, and "electric eyes" (optical eyes), which trigger a dead stop when an object breaks their light path. Paper on the bed or table does not interrupt the optical sensor's light path.

FOLDING

Sheet Folding

Books, magazines, and pamphlets consist of sections called **signatures.** When printed on a sheetfed press, the signature starts out as a single large sheet onto which many pages are printed. After printing, the sheet is folded down to untrimmed page size. Some or all of the folds may be trimmed off later. The folding is usually accomplished on a buckle folder, a knife folder, or a folder that features both. Other jobs that require folding include maps and mass mailings.

Parallel folds and **right-angle folds** are common folding sequences. In parallel folding, all subsequent folds are parallel to the first fold. In right-angle folding, at least one subsequent fold is at right angles to the first one. A variety of configurations can be made using these two basic folds, including accordion folds, signature folds, gate or panel folds, French folds, and letter folds.

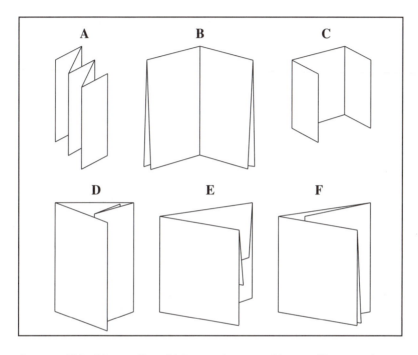

Common folds: (a) accordion, (b) 8-page signature, (c) gate, (d) over-and-over, (e) French (heads in), and (f) letter.

The **knife folder,** which is best suited to right-angle folding, and the **buckle folder,** which is best suited to parallel folding,

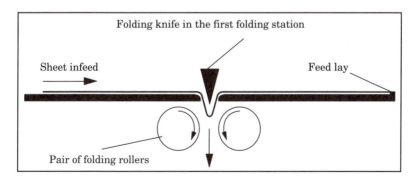

Knife folding. *Courtesy Heidelberg USA, Inc.*

are the folding machines used most often. Both can be equipped to perforate, slit, and paste.

Knife folders are constructed in three or four levels that are set at right angles to each other. Some models have additional parallel sections on at least one of the levels. After a sheet is fed into the folder, moving tapes pass it into the first fold level. It is stopped by a gauge and positioned against a side guide. The folding knife then thrusts the sheet between two counter-revolving rollers. The folded sheet is then moved down to the next level. Canvas tapes move it to the next fold station. The process is repeated until the desired number of folds have been made.

Buckle folders use diagonal rollers to position the paper against the side guide and move it to the folding mechanism. For each fold, two feed rollers push the sheet between two metal plates collectively called a **fold plate.** The sheet encounters a stop placed in a preset position inside the fold plate and begins to buckle at the entrance of the fold plate. A third roller and the bottom feed roller seize the buckle and pull it between them. These two rollers act as the feed rollers to the next fold plate, which is inverted.

Some folders use both fold plates and knives. In the most common configurations, the first section consists of several fold plates, and subsequent levels contain right-angle folding knives.

Buckle folding is used for thinner work, the knife folder for thicker work. Consequently, the buckle folder might be the first, second, or third fold; and the knife, the fourth fold.

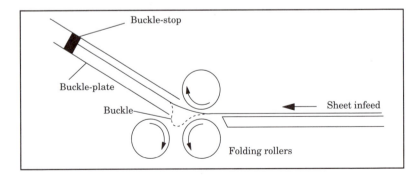

Buckle folding.

Buckle folder.   *Courtesy McCain-Brehmer*

Web Combination Folding

Most web offset presses are equipped to deliver a folded product or signature. Folder choice is dependent on the nature of the work to be produced. Page size and format, number of pages, and grain direction requirements in the finished product are primary considerations. The production speed and degree of flexibility needed for varying the number of pages in the signatures are also important.

Kinds of folds. The grain of the paper always runs in the direction of web travel. **Former folds** and **chopper folds** are made parallel to the grain; **jaw folds** are always made across the web at right angles to the grain.

A former fold is created when the web is pulled over the nose of a triangular metal former board. This folds the web in half—in the direction of web travel. Many folders are arranged to first make a former fold in the web, followed by additional folds. In some specialized folders, only a former fold is made, followed by a knife cutoff and delivery.

In a jaw fold, the paper web flows around a cylinder and is tucked into the jaws of a second cylinder by the first cylinder's tucker blade. A knife in the same set of cylinders cuts the web into individual signatures. If a second jaw fold is made, a double-parallel folded signature is the result.

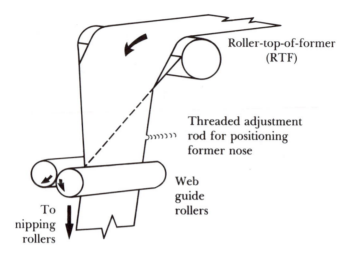

The former board and related elements.

A chopper fold, or quarter fold, when employed, is the final folding operation. After jaw folding, the signature is conveyed in a horizontal plane with the folded edge forward. It passes under a blade that chops the signature between two rotary folding rollers. The backbone or spine fold thus made is parallel to the paper grain. Chopper folding speeds are normally somewhat limited in comparison to other folds because the method by which

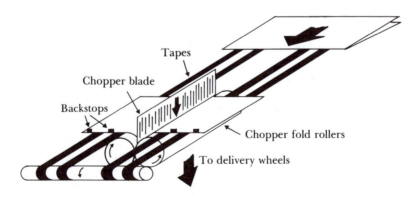

Chopper fold mechanism.

the paper folds does not permit maintaining a positive grip on the signature. For this reason, high-production chopper folders employ a more sophisticated method of dividing the stream of signatures leaving the jaw fold section. Using one or more pairs of choppers, they output more signatures per hour. Multiple chopper folders deliver signatures in two or four streams.

Combination folder. The combination folder is so named because it combines former, jaw, and chopper folding in one

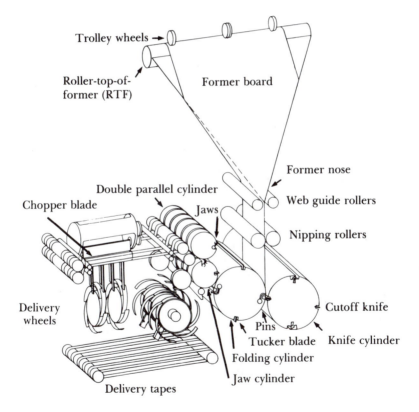

Typical combination folder.

machine. It broadens the versatility of the press, delivering one stream of signatures at a time—all identical in size, format, and paging. More specialized folders that deliver one size of signature with variability in the number of pages are also available.

The popularity of the combination folder is attributed to its versatile folding capability. Primarily designed for web widths in the customary 34–40-in. (866–1,016-mm) range, a combination folder delivers tabloid signatures (eight pages per web), double digest signatures (thirty-two pages per web, or sixteen pages—two-up), and magazine-size signatures (sixteen pages per web).

ASSEMBLING

Most books and magazines have many signatures. After they are folded, they are assembled by gathering, inserting, and, sometimes, collating. Gathering is the method used to assemble signatures that are to be adhesive-bound or sewn. Signatures are assembled one on top of another in proper sequence.

When a printed product is to be saddle-stitched, signatures are inserted by assembling one inside another in a predetermined sequence. Unlike gathering, inserting can be the complete assembly, including cover, of soft-covered items. If the cover is printed together with other parts, a book is said to be self-covered. A book is covered, or plus cover, if its cover is printed separately, generally on a heavier stock.

Collating, another method of assembly, involves stacking individual cut pages one on top of the other. Collating is often used in assembling loose-leaf or mechanically bound books. It differs from gathering in that it involves single sheets or pages while gathering involves signatures.

BINDING

Several kinds of binding methods exist: wire stitching, adhesive binding, case binding, and mechanical binding.

Wire Stitching

Wire-stitched items are characterized by wire stitches that resemble staples through either their centerfolds (**saddle-stitching)** or their sides (**side stitching**).

The term "saddle stitching" comes from the saddle-like device over which the folded signatures hang while being stitched. The stitcher heads are fed from continuous rolls of wire. The cover and the body signatures of the publication are bound at the same time.

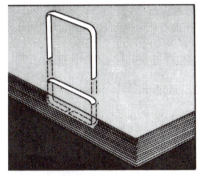
Side stitch

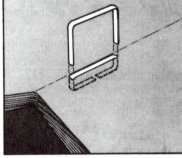
Saddle stitch

Types of wire stitching.

Saddle binder.   *Courtesy Muller Martini, Inc.*

Saddle-stitched signatures are **inserted** into each other as they are carried along the saddle or rail prior to stitching. Trimming the top, bottom, and front edges of the piece usually follows stitching. The in-line combination of automatic inserters, saddle stitchers, and trimmers is very common for the binding of magazines and pamphlets. Numbering, addressing, and other in-line operations can be included at the delivery end of the trimmer.

Side stitching, which is used less often than saddle stitching, involves fastening wire staples through the side of a book parallel to its binding edge (backbone), resulting in a square back. It is particularly well-suited for binding thick publications.

Adhesive Binding

Adhesive binding is sometimes called **perfect binding**. In bookbinding, signatures to be adhesive-bound are first gathered. Next, the backbone is cut and roughed, exposing the edge of each sheet for the next step, which is gluing. The sheets are then glued together at their binding edges. The cover is wrapped around the backbone and glued to the body. Hot-melt plastic

RG/UB adhesive binder.   *Courtesy AM Graphics*

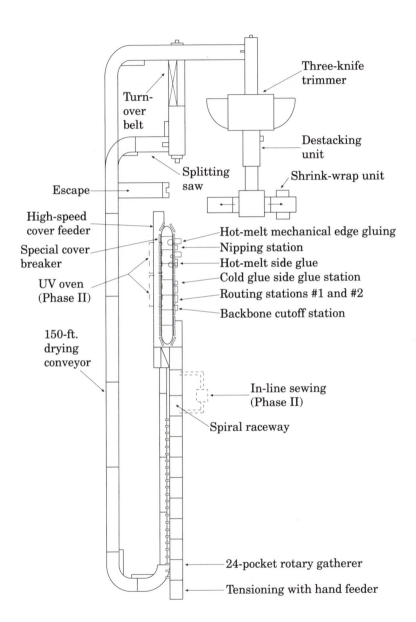

Diagram of Otabind Muller Martini adhesive binding line.
Courtesy Muller Martini, Inc.

glues are used because they dry immediately when cooled. Square-back books with a simple wraparound paper cover (paperbacks) are the most common adhesive-bound product. Adhesive-bound books encased in hard covers are casebound.

Sewing

Thread sewing has two major categories: **side sewing,** which involves sewing through the side of the binding edge, and **saddle sewing,** or sewing through the centerfold. Saddle sewing is similar to saddle stitching in wire stitching in that the signatures are carried to the sewer on a saddle, but the term saddle sewing is seldom used. Sewers are often referred to by the brand name of the most popular machine, i.e., the Singer saddle sewer, which sews through the centerfold of single-signature books; and the Smyth sewer, which uses through-the-centerfold threads not only to hold the sheets of the signature together but also to link the signatures to one another.

Side sewing provides a very strong binding. Manual side sewing is used most often for library and repair work. Machine side sewing with a single thread, sometimes called **McCain sewing,** is a fast system suitable for production work. A needle carries thread through drilled holes and a looper in a square stitch pattern. Double-thread sewing, called **Singer side sewing,** uses a needle and bobbin system similar to household sewing machines except that the holes are punched for the needle. It is often used for repair work.

Singer saddle sewing joins only the pages of single-signature books together at the centerfold. A linked-signature saddle sewing system called **Smyth sewing** was developed for the saddle sewing of books with multiple signatures.

During Smyth sewing, the thread is carried in several parallel rows through the centerfold of each signature and also from one signature to the next. This network of threads binds the pages of each signature together and binds the signatures to each other.

Several sets of stitches—up to six—are along the book's backbone. For each set of stitches, two holes are punched through the centerfold. A needle carries the thread down through one hole while a hook descends through the other. A looper moving inside the signature engages the thread near the needle's eye and carries a loop of it to the hook. The needle and hook rise, the hook pulling the loop through the hole and through the loop from the preceding signature. The sewn signature is pushed back and the next signature is placed in sewing position on the saddle. This operation forms a continuous string of stitched and linked signa-

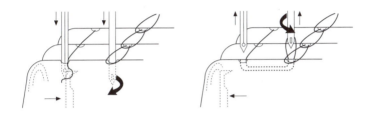

Principle of Smyth sewing.

tures. In semiautomatic machines, the signatures are hand-fed to the saddle and the machine operations. Semiautomatic machine operations activated by foot pedal include sewing, attaching the first signature to the second and the next-to-the-last to the last with a strip of paste, and cutting the thread between books. In fully automatic machines used in production lines, the gathered books are inserted into a feeding station, and all operations are performed automatically.

Before the gathered books can be covered, they must be **nipped,** which is clamping or squeezing to reduce the swell caused by stitching. "Nipping" is also referred to as *smashing* when soft, bulky papers are involved.

CASE BINDING

Case binding can be divided into three different categories: **edition binding, job binding,** and **library binding.** These terms refer to the quantity and the nature of the binding. Edition binding is the binding of casebound books in relatively large quantities. Because edition binders use mostly automatic and semiautomatic equipment, they rarely handle runs smaller than 1,500.

Job binding is the binding of small quantities of casebound books. It involves considerable amounts of handwork and is also used for books that cannot be handled by automatic equipment, such as Bibles and prayer books bound in limp leather.

Library binding is a special service rendered to libraries and includes prebinding, rebinding, and general repair work. Library binders, like job binders, deal with small quantities and use considerable handwork. The main purpose of library binding is to provide books that are sturdy enough to withstand the wear and tear to which books are exposed in public libraries.

Casebound, or cased-in, books are typical hardbound books. The covers, called **cases,** are rigid or flexible boards covered on the outside and on the edges (referred to as **"covers-turned-over-boards"**) with cloth, leather, or other material. The boards for cases are cut first by a machine that slits a large board into strips and then by another machine that crosscuts the strips to book board size. Casemaking machines are fed boards completely cut to size; some of them accept covering material (such as cloth) in web form, while others accept only precut cover blanks. The casemaking machine automatically glues the covering material, affixes boards and backlining paper in place, turns the covering material in over the boards, and presses the completed cover. Covers are often preprinted, most commonly by offset lithography. Other covers are stamped with ink, foil, or genuine gold after casemaking, instead of, or in addition to, preprinting.

Precovering Operations

Books are given the following treatments (some of which are optional) before merging with the cover-making line.

Rounding. Rounding improves a book's structure by giving it a convex binding edge and concave fore-edge. This is achieved by running the book binding-edge-forward between steel rollers rotating in opposite directions. Side-stitched or side-sewn books cannot be rounded.

Backing. Backing—clamping the book and flaring the back outward from the center over the clamped edges—provides greater

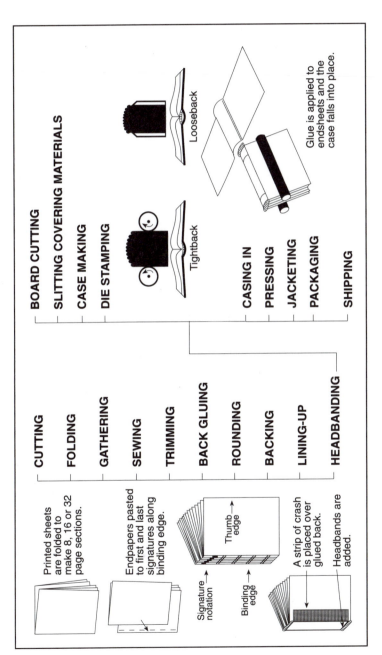

BOARD CUTTING

SLITTING COVERING MATERIALS

CASE MAKING

DIE STAMPING

Looseback

Tightback

Glue is applied to endsheets and the case falls into place.

CASING IN

PRESSING

JACKETING

PACKAGING

SHIPPING

CUTTING

Printed sheets are folded to make 8, 16 or 32 page sections.

FOLDING

GATHERING

Endpapers pasted to first and last signatures along binding edge.

SEWING

TRIMMING

Signature notation

Binding edge

Thumb edge

BACK GLUING

ROUNDING

BACKING

LINING-UP

A strip of crash is placed over and glued back.

HEADBANDING

Headbands are added.

Sequence of casebinding operations.

flexibility and permanence for the rounded back and the ridges that the hinged covers swing against. Rounding and backing are parts of the same machine operation.

Back gluing. To keep the binding edge even, and to maintain its rounded shape after rounding and backing, the binding edge is coated with glue or a flexible resin film.

Backlining. Crash or super, a cloth material made of long, strong fibers and stiff kraft paper, is glued to the backbone of books after they have been rounded and backed.

Head banding. Head and tail bands are often used as a decorative touch. They may be attached to the paper lining before it is glued to the back, or to the book itself.

Edge treatments. Most books do not receive any edge treatments, but occasionally one or more edges are stained or gilded. Most other edge treatments, such as marbling, are now very rare.

THE COVERING PROCESS

The covering process consists of two operations, **casing-in** and **building-in.** Casing-in attaches the cover to the body of the book. The free halves of the four-page end papers are coated on the outside with paste. The case is placed over the book in such a way that when the covers are pressed against the end papers, the edges of each cover will project uniformly beyond the edges of the end papers. A loose-back casing-in does not glue the book's backbone to the cover, which permits the back part of the cover to curve out from the backbone when the book is opened. Some books, mostly those side-sewn or side-stitched, are given a tight-back casing-in with glue on the backbone.

Building-in refers to drying the adhesive that glues the end papers to the cover boards. In small operations, the books are placed around the edges of a wooden board, backs outward, with the cover's joint resting on a brass strip fastened to the edge of the board. Stacks of boards and books in alternating layers are held under pressure for a period of time, often overnight.

Building-in machines hold the cased-in book between pressing plates that apply pressure and heat. With such equipment, building-in can be accomplished in less than a minute while the book is moving through the machine.

In-line equipment for high-volume work combines all of the forwarding and covering operations—rounding, backing, casing-in, building-in, and even jacketing—into one completely mechanized production line.

Mechanical Binding

Mechanical binding is the joining of individual leaves of paper with an independent binding device. Products that are often mechanically bound include advertising and sales literature, stationery items, calendars, and cookbooks.

Loose-leaf binding. Loose-leaf binding is characterized by a binding device that is almost always riveted into or otherwise attached to a fairly sturdy cover. Looseleaf-bound pages are interchangeable.

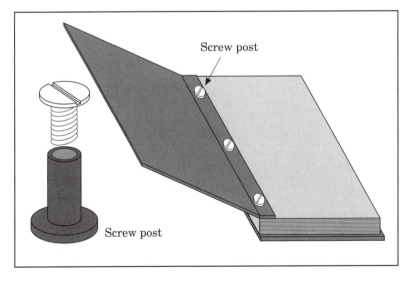

Loose-leaf binding with a screw post binding device.

Spiral binding. Spiral binding requires threading a wire or plastic coil into prepunched holes. The coil insertion may be performed by hand, started by hand and completed by pressing the coil against a revolving rubber cylinder, or accomplished by automatic insertion machines. Wire-O system binding is a type of spiral binding.

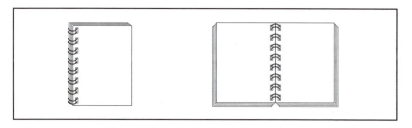

Spiral binding.

Plastic comb binding. Plastic comb binding is often referred to as *GBC binding*. It is applied in two stages. First, the collated booklet is punched with holes along the spine, and then the plastic comb is mechanically inserted into the holes and locked in position. GBC is an acronym for the General Binding Corporation.

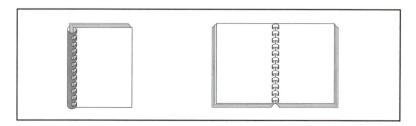

Comb binding.

Covers for mechanical binding may be two-piece, with the book's backbone exposed; one-piece, with scored wraparounds that are punched or slotted in the backbone to accommodate the binding device; or semiconcealed, which means that when the covers are closed, they completely conceal the mechanical binding.

Two-piece covers can be gathered in the same operation with other sheets of the book. They can be self-covers that are printed at the same time and on the same stock as the main body of the book, but more commonly, covers are of a heavier stock. One of the advantages of collated books is that the body leaves can be freely mixed stocks. Most mechanically bound books are collated in this way.

The wraparound covers in semiconcealed binding must be put in place after the pages have been assembled, but before the binding is accomplished. Some semiconcealed bindings use covers that are constructed of boards or other materials and may be as well crafted as those of any edition binding. These semiconcealed binding covers are applied in a separate operation similar to the methods used for other hardcover books.

Trimming

The trimming operation follows the binding operation in every process except mechanical and loose-leaf binding and casing in of casebound books. Trimming brings the bound material to its exact predetermined dimensions, or trim size, with cleanly even edges. Trimming also removes the closed edges of folded signatures and separates magazines bound two- or three-up (two or three copies connected end to end).

Saddle-stitched and adhesive-bound publications are trimmed on the head, front, and bottom edges. Trimming is done with cutting machines or multiknife trimmers.

When trimming is performed in line with binding, it is done with a three-, four-, or five-knife trimmer that trims three sides of the book (or two or three books) in two or three successive cuts.

Cutters. Smaller general-purpose guillotine cutters are used for trimming small quantities because they are more convenient for the operator. The three-part split back gauges on some guillotine cutters allow different parts of the cutters to be set for trimming the tail, the front, and the head of the bound book.

A special model of guillotine cutter has its movable gauge in front of the cutting blade. This makes it easier to load narrow books for trimming.

Multiknife trimmers. The duplex cutter, which cuts two sides at a time, was the first multiknife cutter/trimmer. Three-knife machines combine operations to trim three sides in this order: front, head, and tail (or vice versa). Two- and three-up books require additional blades. In a continuous operation, the operator feeds piles of untrimmed books into one side, and completely trimmed books are delivered at the other; the machine may be trimming the front of one stack of books while trimming the ends of another. When trimming is part of a finishing sequence having other in-line operations, the bound material is fed automatically from the binder into the trimmer.

FINISHING

Embossing

Embossing is the process of creating relief or raised images on printed paper, blank paper, or other flat material in order to create a design or aesthetic enhancement. Embossed images that are not also foil-stamped, tinted, or inked is **blind embossed.** *Debossing,* the opposite of embossing, is the lowering of a surface.

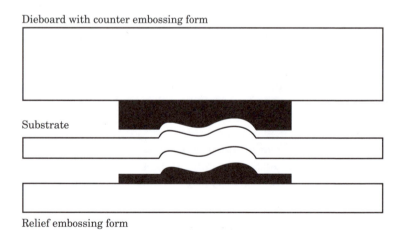

Dieboard with counter embossing form

Substrate

Relief embossing form

Typical embossing configuration.   *Courtesy Bobst*

In addition to creating designs, embossing is used in label printing to stretch the fibers of the paper labels, which eliminates the effects of grain direction, thereby increasing the flexibility of the paper and making it easier to apply them to curved surfaces, such as bottles and cans.

Roller embossing and **plate embossing** are the two main methods of embossing paper. Roller embossing, or *pebbling,* is used in paper mills to produce an overall pattern on paper. Plate embossing is used for individual unit patterns. Roller embossing is done on a rotary machine having two rollers. The embossing roller is an engraved steel roller, its mate a smooth cotton or papier-maché roller. The paper is run between both rollers, and by adjusting the pressure, the desired depth of embossing is produced. Eggshell, moiré, stucco, and linen are some commonly used pebbling designs.

Plate embossing is used for labels, letterheads, book covers, business cards, and many other products. In plate embossing, such images and designs as medals, flowers, company logos, type, scrolls, and frames are produced. Plate embossing is done on a press that has two parallel surfaces; a bed and a platen. The relief embossing die is mounted on a base that is clamped to the bed of the press. The counter die is attached to the platen, which also receives the paper. Embossing is accomplished by placing paper over the counter die then bringing the bed and platen together, exerting enough pressure to force the paper into the relief die.

Relief embossing dies. Magnesium and brass are the two materials that are used most often to make embossing and foil stamping dies. Magnesium, which is less expensive than brass, is generally used for jobs that need to be produced quickly. While adequate for single-level embossing, magnesium dies do not have the bevels, hand finishing, and sculpturing that brass dies have. These characteristics of a brass die make it more suitable for high-quality embossing. Both magnesium and brass dies are generally ¼ in. (6 mm) high.

Counter dies. In order to get the desired result from an embossing operation, the relief die must have a perfectly matched counter die. The relief die is mounted on the die heating plate that is clamped in the bed of the press; the counter die is then mounted in register on the platen.

Counter dies can be made from several materials by various methods. The press operator can cast a hard, durable counter die by using a counter-cast resin material to form it. A die made from such a material will last for long runs with few adjustments. Counter dies can also come precast from the die maker.

Foil Stamping and Foil-Stamped Embossing

Foil-stamped products can be **flat-stamped,** which means that they do not show a surface emboss. Foil-stamped embossed, or

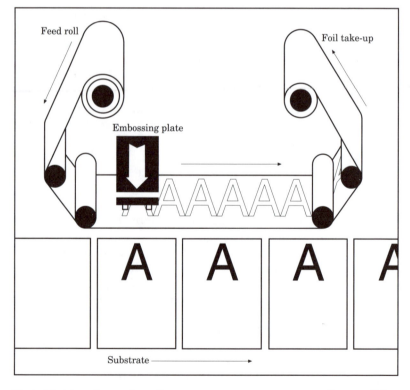

Typical hotstamping configuration. *Courtesy Bobst*

foil embossed, items are embossed and stamped with foil in the same operation. Debossing can also be done with foil. The end result is a **foil deboss.** Foil is commonly stamped on letterheads, business cards, and covers for books. However, greeting card manufacturers and carton stampers use this process the most.

KLUGE 14×22-in. EHE series foil-stamping, embossing, and diecutting press. *Courtesy Brandtjen & Kluge, Inc.*

Diecutting

Two kinds of dies—steel rule and high or hollow—are used to diecut paper, cardboard, and other sheet material. Steel rule dies are used for very intricate shapes. In most cases, they are used for single sheet cutting as they can rarely cut more than five to ten sheets at a time.

High or hollow dies are made of cold-rolled steel that is forged and welded to the required shape. High-dies vary in height. They must not be higher than 2⅜ in. (60 mm) or lower than 1⅜ in. (35 mm); they may be as small in area as 1×1 in. (25.4×25.4 mm) and as large as 6×6 in. (152×152 mm). Their inside is parallel for approximately 1-in. (25.4-mm) height; beyond that height, the inside of the die may funnel out. From this description, you can see why the term high-die or hollow die is used for them. High-dies can be used on open presses having two flat surfaces. In one kind of press, such as a punch press, the die moves and the stack of paper to be cut is stationary. In other presses, the die is stationary and the paper stack is moved into position.

Steel rule diecutting is a stamping process in which cardboard and many other stocks can be cut, scored, and creased, to assume almost any desired shape. Steel rule dies are made to fit the design of a carton or cardboard display.

A steel rule die must be custom-made for each job. The steel rule die combines several functions—cutting, scoring, and punching—in one operation. A steel rule die is a cutting tool consisting of three materials: steel, rubber, and plywood. The steel cuts and scores, the rubber pushes the cut pieces away from the die, and the wood acts as a base for the steel and rubber.

The shape of the carton is cut into the plywood base—known as the dieboard—with a jigsaw or laser. The cutting and scoring rules are bent and shaped and then inserted in the saw-tracks or laser cuts.

9 Paper

Although numerous substrates are printed upon, paper is by far the most popular. It is one of the costliest materials in printing and often determines the success of a printed piece. The following sections will discuss paper manufacture, important paper properties, paper requirements for various printing processes, and paper weights and paper sizes (basis weight and basic size). Different kinds of paper and the end-products for which they are most often used will also be described.

PAPER MANUFACTURE

Raw Materials

The principal raw material used in papermaking is wood fiber obtained from trees or recycled paper. Cellulose fibers have a very high tensile strength and a great affinity for water, meaning that they can be bonded together strongly in a network to form paper. The size and shape of fibers, which vary with the type of tree and even within a given tree, have an important influence on paper properties.

Other plants, such as sugarcane, esparto, and bamboo, are also used as fiber sources. Nonwood plants, such as cotton and linen, are only a minor source of fiber for papermaking in general; however, many nonwood fibers are important to the manufacture of high-quality, fine-textured writing papers.

In addition to a fiber that can network with other fibers to form a sheet, a wide variety of nonfibrous substances are added during papermaking to alter a paper's properties. Fillers are added to increase opacity and brightness and reduce ink show-through. They also reduce a paper's bulk, increase smoothness, make paper more uniformly receptive to printing inks, improve printability, and contribute to greater dimensional stability. Clay, titanium dioxide, and calcium carbonate are the most commonly used fillers.

Dyes and colored pigments are other paper additives. They are used to tint white papers and produce colored papers.

Pulping Methods

The papermaking process begins with harvesting trees. The trees are cut into logs 4–8 ft. (1–2 m) long. Their bark is removed and the logs are then chipped into 1-sq.in. (25-mm^2) chips for pulping. Pulping separates wood fibers from the wood chips forming individual fibers, which become pulp. The three basic pulping methods are mechanical, chemical, and a combination of mechanical

Trees being harvested.   *Courtesy Glatfelter Pulpwood Co.*

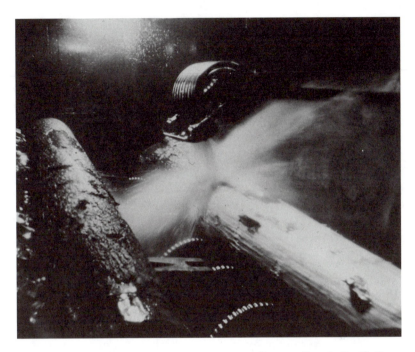

Hydraulic debarking.   *Courtesy Georgia-Pacific Corp.*

Two-pocket grinder makes groundwood pulp.   *Courtesy Montague Machine Co.*

and chemical pulping treatments. Each method produces pulp
that imparts different properties to paper. The chemical process
is the most widely used. Caustic soda and sodium sulfide is

mixed with water to form a cooking liquor that is heated to a high temperature and mixed with the chips in a large tank called a digester. The cooking removes the lignin, which is a glue-like substance that holds the wood fibers together, forming wood pulp.

Bleaching of pulp. Unbleached wood pulp ranges in color from cream to dark brown; a brown paper bag is made of unbleached pulp. After washing the brown pulp, it is bleached in stages where impurities are removed. Bleaching the pulp makes the resulting paper whiter, which improves printing contrast. Whiter pulps produce colored papers that are more brilliant.

Paper Machine

The paper machine converts the furnish (a mixture of fibrous pulp and nonfibrous fillers, such as clay, calcium carbonate, and titanium dioxide) into paper.

In the wet or forming section of the paper machine, the diluted furnish, which is 99% water, is pumped onto an endless, fine screen wire conveyor, from which most of the water is removed by gravity or vacuum. The removal of water forms the furnish into a continuous mat of fibers that align themselves randomly in the direction of web flow giving the paper a grain direction. In a fourdrinier paper machine, the bottom of the fiber mat is in contact with the finely woven wire mesh screen, which is made of bronze or plastic material, and called the **wire side.** The top side of the fiber mat is called the **felt side.** The felt side has shorter fibers and more fillers, contributing to the two-sidedness of paper produced on a fourdrinier machine. In a twin-wire paper machine, the paper is formed between two converging wire belts, with water being drained through both sides of the sheet. As a result, the paper does not exhibit two-sidedness. At this point the paper is still 80% water. If a watermark is required, it is done in this section with a raised design on a roll called the dandy roll. The dandy roll presses against the web of paper causing fiber displacement, which is seen as a watermark on dried paper.

Paper machines also have a press section, where as much of the remaining water as possible is removed from the web by

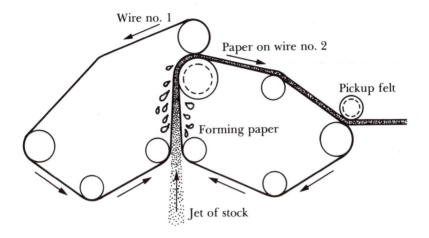

Bel Baie twin-wire former.

pressing and suction, and a drying section, where the remaining water is removed by evaporation caused by hot drying cylinders. Paper leaving the dryer has a moisture level from 2 to 8%, depending on its desired end use.

A paper machine also has a calender, a series of all-metal rollers running in contact that evens out the thickness of the paper, increases its density, and makes it smoother.

Finishing

In papermaking, finishing refers to operations that begin at the end of the paper machine and conclude when the paper is packaged for shipment.

Supercalendering is a method of producing a very high gloss surface on paper stock by passing the sheet between a series of heated metal rollers under pressure. The supercalender has both metal and soft, resilient rolls. The hard metal rolls press into the resilient rolls at the nip, producing a polishing action that imparts varying degrees of smoothness and gloss to the paper.

Embossing gives paper a pattern finish. Like a supercalender, the embosser consists of a metal roll that presses against a soft-surfaced roll. Unlike the supercalender, the metal roll carries an embossed pattern, which is imparted on the soft-surfaced roll through direct running. Paper passing through the nip between these two rolls receives the embossed pattern.

Coating

Coatings are applied to the surface of paper to modify it for various end-use requirements. Coated papers are classified according to their relative gloss: **dull, matte,** or **glossy**. Dull-coated papers are best for reading materials whereas glossy papers are best for reproduction of fine halftones and/or four-color work.

The two principal coating materials are pigments and adhesives, or *binders*. Pigments are used to cover the fibers and obtain a smoother surface. Highly refined clay is the most commonly used pigment. Adhesives bind the pigment particles together and to the paper substrate. They also control final coating properties, such as ink absorptivity, water resistance, and gloss.

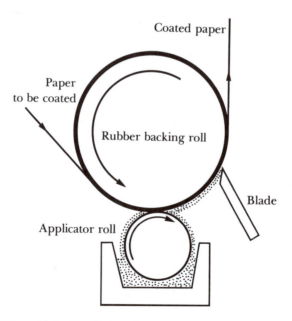

Blade coating with trailing-blade coater.

Coating is applied by systems of many different designs and configurations. The **blade coater** and **air knife coater** are two types of coaters. The blade coater applies a surplus coating to a paper web and then evenly levels and distributes it with a flexible steel blade. The air knife coater applies excess coating to paper and removes the surplus by impinging a flat jet of air upon the fluid coating, leaving a smooth, metered film on the paper. Coating can also be applied **on machine,** which means that it is done at the paper machine, in line with papermaking.

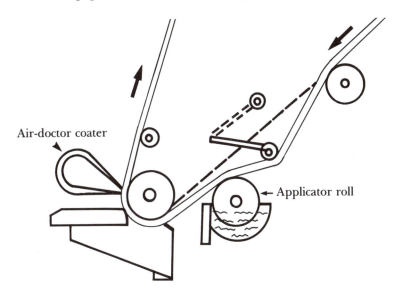

Air-doctor coater

Applicator roll

Air knife coater.

PAPER PROPERTIES

Some papers, because of their combination of properties, may be suitable for only one printing process, while others may be suitable for two or more. Paper properties that are especially important are **gloss, opacity, grain direction,** and **ink absorbency:**
- **Gloss** is the reflectance of light from a smooth paper's surface.
- **Opacity** is the extent to which a paper's ability to transmit light is obstructed.

- **Grain direction** refers to the direction in which the paper's water-suspended fibers were flowing onto the moving paper machine wire. Paper is either **grain long** or **grain short**. With grain-long paper, the grain parallels the long dimension of the press sheet. With grain-short paper, the grain parallels the short dimension The grain direction of a paper is indicated on its label or in boldface type or underlined in the paper catalog.
- **Ink absorbency** determines the rate at which printed ink penetrates the paper.

PAPER WEIGHT

The weight of paper is designated as **basis weight** or **grammage.** Basis weight is the weight, in pounds, of a ream of paper cut to its **basic size,** in inches. With few exceptions, a ream is 500 sheets.

Basic size is the sheet size in inches of a particular type of paper. Basic sizes have been adopted because of widespread practice and use. Following are five common basic sizes:

Paper Type	U.S. Sheet Size	Metric Sheet Size
Bond and writing	17×22 in.	432×559 mm
Cover	20×26	508×660
Newsprint	24×36	610×914
Book	25×38	635×965
Index	25½×30½	648×775

Basis weight is sometimes specified per 1,000 sheets. If so, the basic weight is typically followed by a capital M, representing 1,000 sheets. For example, a particular bond paper having a basis weight of 20 lb. would be designated "40M," indicating that 1,000 sheets weigh 40 lb. The weight of paperboard is per 1,000 sq. ft.

In the metric system, grammage is used to express the weight of paper. Grammage is the weight in grams of a single sheet of paper having an area of 1 m^2. Grammage is abbreviated as g/m^2. (For the sake of reference, note that one pound equals 454 g, and one meter equals 39.37 in.)

Conversion factors are used to convert basis weight to grammage, and vice versa, as the following table shows:

Basic ream size	To convert from grammage to lb./ream, multiply g/m² by:	To convert from lb. to g/m², multiply lb./ream by:
17×22 in.	0.266	3.76
20×26	0.370	2.70
20×30	0.427	2.34
22×28	0.438	2.28
22½×28½	0.456	2.19
25½×30½	0.553	1.81
23×35	0.573	1.74
24×36	0.614	1.62
25×38	0.675	1.48

Caliper and Bulk

The thickness of paper and paperboard is commonly described as **caliper.** Thickness in English units is reported in thousandths of an inch or in points where each point equals one thousandth of an inch. In the metric system, thickness is expressed in milli-meters or micrometers (one thousandth and one millionth of a meter respectively).

International Paper Sizes

The table and illustration on the following page exemplify inter-national "A" paper sizes. In this system, a full-stock trimmed-sheet size is designated "A0." It measures 33⅛×46¾ in., or 841×1189 mm. Progressive divisions of the "A0 sheet" are obtained by halving the sheet across its longest edge. A1 is 23½×33⅛ in., and A2 is 16½×23⅛ in. The smallest division is A7.

KINDS OF PAPER AND PAPERBOARD
USED FOR PRINTING

Numerous kinds of paper and paperboard are used for printing. Paperboard refers to paperlike products having a higher basis weight (grammage), greater thickness, and more rigidity than paper. Normally, paperboard has a thickness of at least 12 points (0.012 in. or 0.30 mm). Grades include unbleached kraft paper-

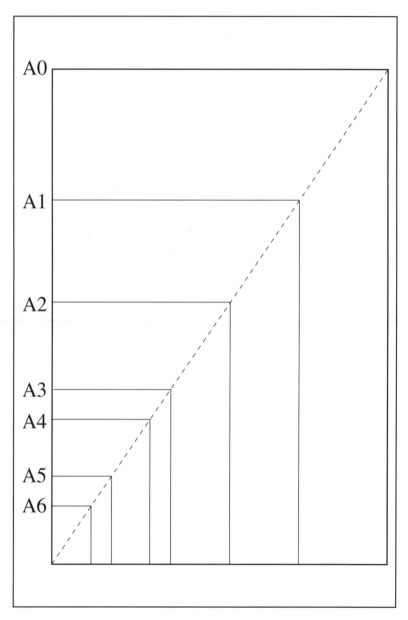

A0 paper chart.

board called solid unbleached sulfate, or SUS, used as a facing material for corrugated containers and for the fabrication of cartons and beverage carriers; recycled paperboard for conversion into containers, folding and set-up boxes, cores, corrugating medium and the manufacture of chipboard; corrugating medium as the fluting material in corrugated containers; and solid white, bleached paperboard, called solid bleached sulfate, or SBS, widely used for packaging food and nonedible products, plates, dishes, and blister packaging.

Adhesive-Coated Papers

Adhesive-coated papers have either an adhesive activated by water or heat or one that is permanently tacky. Gummed papers with water-activated adhesives have either a conventional or dry type of applied gumming. Pressure-sensitive adhesive-coated papers have an adhesive that is permanently tacky at normal temperature and adheres to a surface by contact and applied pressure.

Blanks

Blanks are a thick paperboard designed for printing. The thickness of blanks ranges from 15 to 48 pt. (0.38 to 1.22 mm); it is designated by a ply number. Uncoated blanks may be white-lined on one or both sides for printing. Coated blanks can be coated on one or both sides. Blanks are used for printed signs, point-of-purchase and window displays, posters, and calendar backs.

Bond Papers

Bond papers are classified as writing paper and differ from book or printing papers in several important ways. They must have the following qualities: permanence; durability for handling, folding, and loose-leaf binding; adequate internal and surface hardness for pen-and-ink writing, erasure, and typing; and stiffness as required for letterheads and documents.

Bond papers are made in various grades. In addition to business, professional, and personal stationery, high-quality bond papers are used for insurance policies, certificates, statements, deeds, and long-life documents.

Some bond paper grades are available in colors, and in laid, linen, and other finishes. Standard basis weights for some bond papers, which have a basic size of 17×22 in. (432×559 mm), are 13, 16, 20, and 24 lb./ream (49, 60, 75, and 90 g/m^2).

Business forms bond is a special type of bond made for the specific requirements of manufacturing continuous printed forms.

Bristol Papers

Uncoated printing bristols are made from chemical wood pulp (free of groundwood) in white and colors. Finishes are "smooth" and "vellum." Vellum-finish bristol is widely used for offset lithography because of its higher bulk, pleasing surface, and tendency for fast setting of ink with minimum setoff. Because of their excellent strength and bulk, printing bristols are used for covers. Standard basis weights of bristol papers, which have a basic size of 22½×28½ in. (572×724 mm), are 67, 80, 100, 120, 140, and 160 lb./ream (147, 176, 219, 263, 307, and 351 g/m^2).

Carbonless Papers

Carbonless papers are replacing many carbon interleaved forms since they simplify paperwork, produce clean, smudge-free copies, and eliminate the messiness associated with use and disposal of carbon paper. Carbonless papers are technically different from regular papers. The back side of the top sheet in the carbonless set is coated with encapsulated chemicals, and the front and back sides of intermediate sheets have a receptor coating and an encapsulated coating respectively. The last sheet of the set has a receptor coating only. When pressure is applied to the top sheet of the set by typing, writing, or "crash printing," an image is formed by the reaction between the chemicals liberated from the collapsed capsules and the contacting receptor coating. Special precaution must be taken not to damage the encapsulated chemicals by excessive pressure and friction during handling, printing, cutting, and trimming.

Coated Label Papers

Label papers coated on one side (C1S) are designed for the diverse requirements associated with the manufacture, application, and end use of printed labels. These requirements include the printing process itself; varnishing, lacquering, bronzing, and embossing; the labeling application; laminating or combining with another material; and compatibility with the adhesive used. The coated side of labels may be supercalendered, cast-coated, or matte-finished, as well as white or colored. Labels are used for such applications as box wraps, cigarette packaging, metal can and bottle labels, posters, book jackets, food wraps, pressure-sensitive labels, and lamination to paperboard. Regular basis weights for label papers, which have a basic size of 25×38 in. (635×965 mm), are 60 and 70 lb./ream (89 and 104 g/m^2).

Coated Printing Papers

Coated printing papers are available in a variety of grades and types and are made specially for sheetfed or web offset lithography, gravure, and flexography.

Sheetfed offset lithography. Enamel papers for sheetfed offset are manufactured in various grade levels—sometimes designated as a premium or a grade level number of 1, 2, 3, or 4, depending upon the print quality, gloss, ink holdout, and brightness. Cast-coated paper has an exceptionally smooth, level, ink-absorbent surface, which is produced by a unique casting process, and a mirrorlike gloss. Standard basis weights of enamel papers, which have a basic size of 25×38 in. (635×965 mm), are 60, 70, 80, and 100 lb./ream (89, 104, 118, and 148 g/m^2). Matching cover papers with a basic size of 20×26 in. (508×660 mm) have weights of 65, 80, and 100 lb./ream (162, 175, 216, and 270 g/m^2).

Like the high-gloss enamels, dull-finish enamels are super-calendered, but in a different manner and with coating formulations that result in less gloss. They are used where good ink holdout and a lay of ink approaching that of glossy enamels is wanted, but without a glossy paper background. Dull-finish enamels are used for annual reports, catalogs, product brochures, and books and jobs where high-quality multicolor reproduction with minimal paper gloss is desired.

The fully coated matte types of papers offer distinct advantages to the lithographer. They combine some of the advantages of printing on both uncoated and enamel papers. While they do not have the high degree of ink holdout that an enamel paper has, their lithographic reproduction is far superior to that of uncoated papers. Matte-coated papers have a glare-free background and handle like uncoated paper on press. They generally have a higher bulk and opacity than enamel papers of the same weight, since they are not supercalendered. Standard basis weights for matte-coated papers with a basic size of 25×38 in. (635×965 mm) are 50, 60, 70, 80, and 100 lb./ream (74, 89, 104, 118, and 148 g/m^2) and weights for matching cover, which has a basic size of 20×26 in. (508×660 mm), are 60, 65, and 80 lb./ream (162, 175, and 216 g/m^2).

Web offset. Coated papers for web offset are available in high-gloss enamel, dull-finish enamel, and a matte surface similar to that used for sheetfed offset. However, they are made for the specific requirements of heatset drying and for running on a web press. The upper limit of basis weight generally does not exceed 100 lb. (148 g/m^2) because of blistering and folding problems with heavyweight papers. For basis weights under 50 lb. (74 g/m^2) printed web offset, groundwood coated publication grades are used.

Lightweight coated printing papers. Lightweight coated printing papers, no. 4 but primarily no. 5 groundwood coated grade, are used extensively for high-volume web offset or rotogravure printing of magazines, catalogs, and preprinted newspaper inserts and coupons. Basis weight range is 30 lb. to 40 lb. (44 to 59 g/m^2).

Cover Papers

The primary functions of a cover paper are physical and aesthetic. With regard to physical function, a cover paper must have sufficient strength and durability to protect its contents adequately under normal use. With regard to aesthetic function, the cover must represent its contents in an attractive and appropriate manner as desired by the designer and the customer.

Coated covers are available in white and numerous colors and in different finishes, grades, and basis weights. They include plastic-laminated and pyroxlin-coated covers, which are water, soil, and grease resistant and require special printing inks. Other specialty covers are coated with mica, gold, or silver; have flocked or velour surfaces; or are embossed, i.e., have deeply raised or depressed areas resembling the texture of leather or cloth.

The basic size of cover papers is 20×26 in. (508×660 mm). Basis weights extend from 50 lb./ream (135 g/m^2) to as high as 19-point thickness (0.48 mm).

Latex-treated Papers

Latex-treated papers have their fibrous network impregnated with latex to ensure durability, high-edge tear resistance, wet strength, flexibility, and leatherlike properties. They may be coated for improved printability and resistance to oil, grease, and water. Embossed patterns with leather and fabric designs may be applied. Latex-treated papers can be stretched, stamped, punched, and embossed in the same manner as leather. They are used for rugged printed covers, charts, maps, labels, banners, tags, book covers, and children's books.

Ledger Papers

Ledger papers are made in heavier basis weights than bond papers. Standard basis weights for ledger papers with a basic size of 17×22 in. (432×559 mm) are 24, 28, 32, and 36 lb./ream (90, 105, 120, and 135 g/m^2). Their finish may be smooth or slightly rough, for machine posting of data—known as a "posting finish." Ledger papers must have good strength, stiffness, and a hard surface suitable for pen and ink, erasing, ruling, and data entry. They are made from all-chemical wood pulp, from a combination of wood and cotton fibers, or from 100% cotton fiber. Typical uses are loose-leaf and bound ledger books, accounting record systems, wills, deeds, and other long-lasting documents.

Lightweight Printing Papers

Bible paper, once printed by letterpress only, was the forerunner of lightweight printing papers. Lightweight printing papers, which have a basic size of 25×38 in. (635×965 mm), have exceptionally high opacity for their weight. Their basis weight extends from 17 to 40 lb./ream (25 to 59 g/m^2). Web offset has the advantage over sheetfed printing in the printing of lightweight papers, which is one reason for their increased use. Lightweight papers are suitable for Bibles, handbooks, dictionaries, financial and legal printing, and professional reference books because they reduce bulk and offset some of the increased costs of mailing. The subsequent savings in postage and distribution costs can often far outweigh the high initial costs associated with these papers.

Manifold and Onionskin Papers

Manifold and onionskin papers are essentially lightweight bond papers. Manifold papers are available in a machine or unglazed finish, and in a finish machine-glazed on one side for producing distinct carbon copies. Onionskin papers are air-dried and have a cockle, smooth, or calendered finish. Their fiber content may be all-chemical wood, or 25% or 100% cotton fiber. Regular basis weights for a basic size of 17×22 in. (432×559 mm) are 8 or 9 lb./ream (30 or 34 g/m^2). Manifold and onionskin papers are used for airmail stationery, lightweight reports, catalogs, envelope enclosures, ads, and carbon copies of legal documents.

Newsprint

Newsprint is manufactured largely from groundwood, or other mechanical pulps, specially for the printing of newspapers, which is done by web letterpress, flexography, or web offset.

Parchment

Parchment identifies highly refined, durable, hard-surfaced cotton fiber papers used for etching, drawing, and the printing of wills, deeds, diplomas, stock certificates, and other permanent records.

Safety Papers

Safety papers are able to expose forgery or document alterations made by mechanical erasure or chemicals. They must meet rigid specifications of durability as needed in the handling and treatment of bank checks. Safety papers are available with a protective background in various designs and colors. The standard basis weight for safety papers, which are a basic size of 17×22 in. (432×559 mm), is 24 lb./ream (90 g/m^2). While the largest use for safety papers is printed checks, they are also used for many other negotiable documents that need protection against forgery, such as bonds, deposit slips, coupons, tickets, merchandise certificates, certificates of title, warranties, and legal forms. Check paper must have a smooth surface for imprinting sharply defined, unbroken MICR (magnetic ink character recognition) characters and printing pictorial backgrounds. A critical requirement is adequate bursting and tear strength and a maintained rigidity to withstand repeated handling and many passes through high-speed, check-sorting equipment.

Tag Papers

Tag papers, made from long-fiber sulfate pulp, have exceptional strength and are calendered to a smooth, hard finish. They are available in white, manila, and various colors. Coated tag papers are used where better printability is required. Regular basis weights for tag papers, which have a basic size of 24×36 in. (610×914 mm), are 100, 125, 150, 175, 200, and 250 lb./ream (163, 203, 244, 285, 325, and 408 g/m^2). Typical applications are tags, file folders, job tickets, jackets, heavy-duty envelopes, and covers.

Text Papers

Text papers are functional and aesthetically pleasing, offering many opportunities to the graphic designer. They are made in many different finishes and textured surfaces, bright and natural white shades, and many different colors. Some are watermarked and have deckled edges. Text papers have wove, antique, vellum, and felt types of finishes, which may have light, medium, or heavy pattern depths produced on either the paper machine or embossed after papermaking. Many grades are available in matching envelopes and cover weights. Offset lithography has a distinct advantage over other printing processes in being able to print halftones on the textured surface of text papers. The gamut of colors—which includes strong, bright colors and subdued colors and pastels with their many beautiful surfaces—can be used to great advantage by the printer in adding originality, elegance, and visual appeal to a printed product. Examples are programs, announcements, menus, annual reports, and corporate advertising circulars.

Uncoated Groundwood Printing Papers

Uncoated, machine-finish groundwood printing papers are similar to newsprint but have a smoother surface and higher brightness. They are manufactured with various percentages of fillers to enhance their brightness and printability. Printing applications include catalogs, directories, periodicals, bus transfers, waybills, ballots, and paperbacks. Their basis weight range for the basic size of 25×38 in. (635×965 mm) extends from 20 to 45 lb./ream (30 to 67 g/m^2).

Supercalendered uncoated groundwood papers are used increasingly for rotogravure printing. Printing applications include the supplement and magazine sections of Sunday newspapers, magazines, and catalogs.

Uncoated Groundwood-Free Offset Papers

Uncoated groundwood-free offset papers are available in many grades, finishes, colors, and basis weights for both sheetfed and web offset printing. Finishes include various smooth, wove, vellum, antique, and embossed patterns.

Opaque offsets offer extra opacity and brightness over the standard grades. Colored offset lines offer six or more colors. Their uses include the gamut of commercial printing and applications such as personalized computer-generated letters and promotional mailings in the business forms industry. When used for book manufacturing, they may be custom-made to a specified bulk and shade as well as for a specific printing process and binding requirements.

Wedding Papers

Wedding papers are made with a very uniform, closed formation and have a refined surface, without glare. An obvious appearance of quality and the ability to produce sharply engraved characters are two important requirements. Wedding papers are made from all-chemical wood, wood and cotton, or all-cotton fibers. Finishes are vellum, plate, or linen. The common basis weights for the basic size of 17×22 in. (432×559 mm) are 28, 32, 36, and 40 lb./ream (105, 120, 135, and 150 g/m^2), with bristol weights for acknowledgments, announcements, and business cards. In addition to wedding stationery, wedding papers are used for distinctive stationery and commercial announcements and invitations.

PRINTING REQUIREMENTS

The requirements of paper and paperboard are governed by the printing process used, the operations subsequent to printing, and the end use of the printed product. The optical properties of paper for good printing are largely independent of the printing process. For instance, no printing process produces good print quality on the rough, brown surface of corrugated board, while white enamel papers produce good print quality with a variety of processes. This section discusses the paper requirements of the principal printing processes: sheetfed lithography, web offset lithography, gravure, flexography, screen printing, letterpress, electrostatic printing, and ink jet printing.

Sheetfed Offset Lithography

Because it must withstand comparatively tacky ink films, paper for sheetfed offset lithography must have higher surface and internal bonding strength than that used for other processes. Water resistance is needed to prevent softening and weakening, which can cause picking and a transfer of fibers or coating to the blanket; and to avoid excess moisture pickup from the press dampening system, which would cause curl and distinct changes in paper dimension. However, excessive water resistance, such as in plastic-coated papers, presents other problems for printers.

Sheetfed offset lithography also demands an exceptionally clean and strongly bonded surface compared to the other printing processes. This surface is necessary because there is complete contact between the rubber blanket and the paper and the blanket has a tendency to lift all loosely bound material from the paper.

Since offset lithography operates on chemical principles, paper must not release any materials that will react unfavorably with the plate, ink, or dampening system chemistry.

Web Offset Lithography

Many of the requirements for web offset lithography are the same as those for sheetfed offset. However, the paper's grain direction is always in the same direction as web travel.

Coated papers must be formulated at a lower moisture content to resist blistering, which is the formation of a bubble that bulges out on both sides of the web, and to fold without cracking after heatset drying. Remoisturizers are used in heatset to replace moisture after drying. Since web offset inks generally have lower tack, less moisture is used in the web offset printing system. There is less time for the paper to pick up moisture due to the high speed of web presses. Because of this, the pick and moisture resistance for web offset papers need not be as high as that for sheetfed offset papers. Internal strength is required to resist the delamination forces of blanket-to-blanket presses.

For satisfactory runnability, paper webs must be flat enough to pass through the printing nip of the two blanket cylinders without wrinkling or distorting. Rolls that unwind with even tension and flatness across the web and without localized distortion are required for good register and to prevent wrinkling. Rolls free of defects and with proper splicing are essential for good runnability and for minimizing web breaks. Since the paper web is under tension all the way from the infeed to the cutoff stations, minimal uniform mechanical stretch of the web under tension is necessary for good register.

Web offset papers are generally made with a lower moisture content than sheetfed papers. The lower moisture content helps reduce the overall moisture loss and web shrinkage as paper goes through the press. For coated papers, moisture content must be reduced to prevent blistering that is caused when excess moisture in the paper turns to steam in the dryer. As the basis weight (grammage) of coated paper is increased, its moisture content is often reduced to maintain the volume of water vapor at a safe level and to avoid blistering during heatset drying.

Gravure

Gravure prints well on lower quality, lightweight papers. Sheetfed gravure and rotogravure printing each have specific paper requirements. The paper's surface *must* be microsmooth for both. Softness and compressibility are also important, particularly for uncoated papers that are printed sheetfed gravure. Inadequate smoothness and compressibility, and minute surface depressions or voids, prevent ink transfer because small paper areas fail to contact the inked cells of the gravure cylinder. Surface cleanliness is less important than it is for letterpress and offset lithography. For good runnability, rotogravure printing demands rolls that unwind with even tension and flatness across the web and are free from defects that cause web breaks.

Flexography

There are few special paper requirements for flexographic printing. It is adaptable to a wide variety of paper and paperboard. Flexographic inks have very low tack and dry by evaporation, often aided by heat. Picking is not a problem and dryer temperatures need not be as high as for web letterpress and offset printing. Defect-free rolls that feed with even tension are required for flexography as for other rollfed printing processes.

Screen Printing

Screen printing is capable of printing on many different substrates including all types of paper surfaces. Smoothness is not important, except that it may influence ink drying or smudging. Sheet flatness and the absence of distorted edges are required for complete contact of the paper and screen and ink transfer. Dimensional stability and the ability to maintain sheet flatness after exposure to heat for ink drying is essential. Sufficient basis weight (grammage) and bulk are needed so that printed sheets have enough rigidity to prevent them from curling and sagging during drying and to resist the warping effect of heavy ink films.

Letterpress

The major paper requirements for letterpress printing relate to printability. Pinpoint smoothness is the single most important requirement for complete image transfer. Inadequate smoothness, including the presence of microscopic pits or craters in the paper's surface, results in missing or broken halftone dots and incomplete image transfer. Uniform formation and ink absorbency as well as a level surface are essential for an even lay of ink in heavily inked areas and for printing good halftones. Since letterpress prints with heavy ink films, the paper's surface must be sufficiently ink-receptive to avoid excessive spreading of halftone dots under letterpress impression. Compressibility and printing cushion help a paper surface to change under the pressure of letterpress impression and to contact all areas of the printing plate more completely. Impression tolerance is the term sometimes used to describe the relative ease with which a paper receives letterpress images. It refers to the ability of a paper to produce acceptable print quality with impression pressures higher or lower than the optimum. Rough and hard papers have less impression tolerance than smooth papers.

Adequate pick resistance is needed for letterpress inks. Papers for letterpress printing need not be water-resistant. However, many papers printed by letterpress are water-resistant for other reasons. Surface cleanliness is necessary to avoid accumulation of hickeys in printed images.

Supercalendered coated papers or coated papers that have a high finish obtained by other means are required for printing finer screen halftones. Coated papers should have full and even coverage of their fibers for printing sharp halftones and solids without mottle. For heatset letterpress printing, coated papers must be designed to resist blistering and heat degradation.

Electrostatic Printing

Specifications for smoothness, stiffness, porosity, coefficient of friction, and moisture content are required for proper runnability. Related to print quality are smoothness, sheet flatness, and moisture content. An essential property for both satisfactory runnability and good image quality is the paper's electrical resistivity. For these reasons, papers are made for the specific requirements of various electrostatic printing machines.

Ink Jet Printing

Paper for ink jet printing must absorb the vehicle very rapidly and retain the ink colorant at or near its surface with minimum ink spreading and feathering to produce sharp, dense images. Papers with coatings specially formulated for high-speed, high-resolution ink jet printers meet all of the requirements.

10 Ink

A printing ink is a dispersion of a colored solid (a pigment) in a liquid mixture (vehicle), and it is formulated to produce an image on a substrate. In order to make the ink suitable for producing an image on a commercial printing press, additives must be incorporated into the formula. Solutions of dyes in water or other liquids are usually considered to be writing inks, not printing inks, although today ink jet printers use such materials. Some flexographic inks for special applications are also colored with dyes. Dry or liquid toners, such as those used in electrostatic printing, are not usually considered to be printing inks.

Because printing inks must be formulated to carry out specific jobs, attention must be paid to the printing process for which the ink is designed.

Ink Ingredients

Ink is a complex mixture of pigment, varnish or vehicle, and modifier or additives. A pigment is a finely divided solid material that gives an ink color. It can be either opaque or transparent. The body and working properties of an ink depend not only on the type of vehicle and its viscosity, but also on the nature and amount of pigment it contains.

Pigment particles are dispersed in a liquid mixture known as the **ink vehicle.** The nature of the vehicle determines most of the working properties of the ink and some of its optical qualities as well. The vehicle disperses the pigment, and, after drying, bonds the pigment particles to the paper. A variety of substances including synthetic resins and modifications of natural rosin are used in ink vehicles.

The ink manufacturer adds various materials to the ink to make it press-ready for printing. One additive is a *slip compound*

Pigments.

that improves the printed ink film's resistance to abrasion. Waxes are used in the compound, which is either a micronized dry powder or a fine dispersion of several waxes in an appropriate oil vehicle. Wetting agents, which promote the dispersion of pigments in the vehicle, are also added to many inks. The wetting agent selected by the ink manufacturer must be carefully chosen, to avoid excessive emulsification of dampening solution into the ink and other problems.

Setoff, the unwanted transfer of a wet ink film from the surface of one printed sheet to the back of another, is controlled by the addition of antisetoff compounds, which either protect the ink surface or shorten the ink (decreasing its gelling time).

Shortening compounds reduce ink flying, or misting. The addition of a wax compound shortens the ink.

Reducers, such as kerosene or other petroleum solvents, are occasionally added to an ink to soften it and reduce its tack.

Stiffening agents, such as body gum, stiffen an ink that is too soupy and fails to print cleanly and sharply.

Antiskinning agents are antioxidants that counteract the drying of inks so that they do not skin over in the can.

Most sheetfed printing inks benefit from the addition of a drying agent, or drier, which acts as a catalyst to convert a wet ink film to a dry ink film. Drying agents are, most frequently, salts of cobalt and manganese.

PASTE AND LIQUID INKS

Inks can be classified as either paste or liquid (fluid). Paste inks are used for litho, screen, and letterpress printing. Liquid inks are used for flexo and gravure printing. News inks, although they have a lower body (consistency) than commercial offset and letterpress inks, are commonly considered to be paste inks. The ingredients and manufacturing procedures for these two types are significantly different.

Paste Inks

Paste inks may be made by mixing the dry pigment, pigment flushes or dyes, and some additives into the vehicle or varnish. The ink mixture may then be **milled.** Milling is a shearing

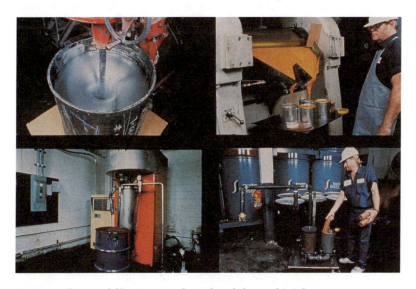

Mixing, milling, and filtering procedures for a lithographic ink.

process that breaks pigments down into fine particles. Mixing and milling are often the only processes necessary for manufacture of paste inks. However, some paste inks are also filtered to remove oversized particles and debris. Depending on the nature of the vehicle, how well the colorant disperses, and the end-use requirement of the ink, the ink may be manufactured exclusively by mixing and filtering.

Lithographic and letterpress inks. Paste inks are used for offset and letterpress printing. The differences between lithographic and letterpress inks are primarily in their formulations (pigment concentration and choice of pigment and varnish) and not in the method of manufacturing them.

Because lithography applies a thinner ink film to the paper than letterpress does, litho inks must be more highly pigmented than letterpress inks.

In addition to the differences in color strength, litho and letterpress inks differ in their sensitivity to water. Although it has been stated that the principle behind lithography is that oil and water do not mix at all, in reality the ink manufacturer must formulate lithographic inks that absorb or pick up some water. Totally water-repellent inks do not work well in lithography.

A typical quickset sheetfed lithographic ink contains pigment, quickset varnish, drier, wax compounds, and solvents. These inks dry primarily by a chemical reaction, a polymerization reaction initiated by oxygen and catalyzed by the drier.

Sheetfed lithographic inks have a higher tack than web inks. Because of the slower speeds of the sheetfed presses, a higher tack is necessary in order to print a sharp dot.

A heatset web offset publication ink contains pigments, heatset varnish, wax compounds, and solvents. The primary drying process for these inks is evaporation as the web goes through the high-velocity hot-air dryer, but absorption and oxidation may also be involved. Chill rollers, located after the dryer, are required to complete the drying process.

Newspaper inks. Black newspaper inks are basically comprised of lamp black pigment and a small amount of blue toner dispersed in mineral oil. The pigment content is low, normally about 10%.

Newspaper printing.

Colored news inks used for printing in the main body of the paper are known as "ROP" (run of press) inks. Most ROP inks are produced by blending mineral oil with pigment flushes, followed by filtering the finished ink.

Low-rub news inks are becoming more popular because they contain drying oils or resins to adhere the pigments to the stock. Conventional news inks do not contain a binder.

Screen printing inks. Screen printing inks usually dry by a combination of solvent evaporation and oxidation. They have a low tack and a thick, nonfluid body so that they can be forced by a squeegee through the stencil screen. Screen inks are similar to paste inks that have been greatly reduced with mineral spirits.

UV inks that dry upon exposure to ultraviolet light are widely used for screen printing.

Liquid Inks

Liquid inks, such as flexo and gravure inks, are easily processed because of their low viscosity. However, they are usually processed in closed containers. The solvents must be highly volatile to dry properly at the low temperatures used for drying on the gravure or flexo presses.

Historically, the ingredients, which consisted of pigment(s), solvent(s), and resin, were mixed in a ball mill. The mixture was then combined with ceramic balls in a large cylindrical vessel or crock. The vessel was tightly closed, turned on its side, and rolled on rollers to mill the ink.

These inks are now manufactured in continuous mills in which the batch flows through a stirring medium consisting of small steel or glass balls or, in rare cases, sand. Because low viscosity allows pigments to settle out, liquid inks are usually formulated at concentrations higher than those needed on the press. The printer dilutes the ink with a suitable solvent at press side. This practice also reduces shipping and storage costs.

Gravure inks. In the manufacture of gravure inks, certain resins are dissolved in solvents and milled with the pigment. The product is filtered, and the refined ink is ready for the printer. Since volatile solvents and flammable resins, such as cellulose nitrate, are involved, provisions must be made against possible fire hazard.

Flexographic inks. Procedures for manufacturing flexographic inks are similar to those for gravure inks. Flexographic inks, like gravure inks, can be produced from chips, which are dispersions of pigments in a dry resin. Since most of the work required to disperse the pigment was done in preparing the chips, only a high-speed mixer is required to make ink from chips.

Technological advances in aqueous liquid inks have opened new markets for water-based flexo inks. Water-based flexo inks contain acrylic resins that give them good pigment wetting characteristics and excellent surface holdout and opacity.

INK FILM THICKNESS

One of the major features affecting the printing processes and the ink formulations for them is the characteristic of the ink film thickness being applied. A thin film of ink requires a higher level of pigmentation (higher color strength) than a thick film. However, thick ink films may actually contain fillers such as clay. In fact, it is often necessary to incorporate a filler into screen inks and letterpress inks—in order to achieve proper flow.

Although the printed ink film thickness applied (by any process) can vary greatly, the following numbers can be considered typical.

Process	mils*	mm	microns
Sheetfed offset	0.2	0.005	5.0
Web offset	0.3	0.008	7.5
Web letterpress	0.4	0.010	10
Gravure	1.2	0.030	30
Screen	1.0–5.0	0.025–0.125	25–125

*A mil is 0.001 in.

For more specific information on printing inks, their uses, and how they are manufactured, consult GATF's *What the Printer Should Know about Ink* book by Nelson Eldred and Terry Scarlett.

Glossary

A

additive color—The color that results when one color of light is added to another, such as by projection onto a white screen.

adhesive-coated paper—Paper that is coated on one side with an adhesive that is either activated by moisture (gummed papers) or heat. It may also be covered with a pressure-sensitive adhesive coating that is permanently tacky at normal temperature and adheres to a surface by contact and applied pressure.

anilox roller—A steel or ceramic ink metering roller on a flexographic press that transfers a thin, controlled ink film from the fountain roller to the rubber printing plate. Tiny, uniform cells engraved on the roller's surface carry the ink.

antisetoff compound—An ink additive that prevents setoff, which occurs when ink from sheets in the delivery pile stick to the backs of other sheets.

antiskinning agent—An ink additive that prevents the ink from forming a skin, or rubbery layer, once it is exposed to air. Also called an *antioxidant.*

ascender—The portion of a lowercase character that extends above the height of its main body. Some examples are seen on the following characters: "h," "k," "b," and "d."

B

backup—A copy of work or information saved in case the original is lost or damaged.

base art—Final layout or comprehensive including all type and line drawings, but not continuous-tone copy.

base sheet—A strong, or heavy, sheet to which typeset copy is adhered, along with artwork, and made into a pasteup, or mechanical.

baseline—The lower boundary of the x-height, which is the height of the main element of a lowercase letter.

basic size—The standard sheet size in inches of a particular type of paper.

basis weight—The weight, in pounds, of a ream of paper cut to its basic size, in inches.

belt press—A printing press with relief printing plates mounted on two continuous tracks for printing books in an in-line operation. The in-line operation begins with a paper roll and ends with a book that is ready to be bound.

bezier curve—In object-oriented computer graphics programs, a shape that is defined by anchor points set along its arc.

bimetal plate—A lithographic printing plate made from two metals, one forming the ink-receptive image area (usually copper) and one forming the water-receptive nonimage area (chromium, stainless steel, aluminum, zinc, etc.).

bindery—A facility where finishing operations, such as folding, gathering, covering, and trimming, are performed.

blank—(1) A thick paperboard, coated or uncoated, produced on a cylinder machine and designed for printing. (2) An unprinted page or sheet side. (3) Unprinted cardboard, metal sheets, or other substrates used for making displays and signs.

blanket cylinder—The large-diameter roller on a lithographic press that carries the offset rubber blanket, placing it in contact with the inked image on the plate cylinder and then placing it in contact with the substrate to offset the ink image.

blanket-to-blanket unit—A perfecting printing unit in which the paper passes between two offset blankets.

body size—The height of a font in metal composition. Also known as *point size,* and expressed in typographic points.

bond paper—A strong, durable writing paper with a smooth, uniform finish, originally used for printing stocks and bonds, now also used for letterheads, stationery, and business forms.

bristol paper—Uncoated printed paper made from chemical wood pulp (free of groundwood). It comes in white and colors and smooth and vellum finishes.

bubble jet—Ink jet technology in which drop emission is produced on demand by a thin film of boiling ink in a tubular chamber. See *drop-on-demand ink jet.*

bulk—The thickness of a pile of an exact number of sheets under a specified pressure.

bulking number—The number of sheets that will bulk 1 in. (25.4 mm). It is used when manufacturing and specifying paper thickness for book manufacturing. To be more practical, bulking number is multiplied by two to give pages per inch since each sheet in a book represents two pages.

C

calender—In papermaking, a series of all-metal rollers running in contact that evens out the thickness of the paper, increases its density, and makes it smoother.

caliper—The thickness of paper and paperboard.

cap height—The height of a capital letter.

capillary system—A photostencil system used in screen printing that consists of a liquid emulsion on a film base. The emulsion, which is coated on a support film, is placed in contact with the wet screen. Pressure applied by hand or by squeegee embeds the emulsion into the screen mesh. After the screen dries, the support film is removed. The screen is then exposed with a light source, washed to remove unexposed areas, and dried.

carbonless paper—A specialty paper that produces duplicate copies of handwritten, typed, or otherwise impact-printed sheets without the use of carbon paper. To achieve this, NCR paper is coated with two different microencapsulated chemicals—one on the face and the other on the reverse side of the sheet. When pressure is applied to two attached sheets, the encapsulated chemicals break and mix, producing a visible image.

cathode-ray tube (CRT)—An electronic vacuum tube with a heated cathode that generates electrons and with multiple grids for accelerating the electrons to a flat screen at the end of the tube. The screen coating fluoresces wherever the electrons strike it, giving off light. CRTs are used as monitors in video display terminals (VDTs) and as an output light source in third-generation phototypesetters.

CCD array—A group of light-sensitive recording elements often arranged in a line (linear array) and used as a scanner image-sensing device. See *charge-coupled device.*

CEPS—Color electronic prepress system.

charge-coupled device (CCD)—A component of an electronic scanner that digitizes images. It consists of a set of image-sensing elements (photosites) arranged in a linear or area array. Images are digitized by an external light source that illuminates the source document, which reflects the light through optics onto the silicon light sensors in the array. This generates electrical signals in each photosite proportional to the intensity of the illumination.

chill rollers—The section on a web offset press where heatset inks are cooled below their setting temperature. It is located after the dryer.

choke—A camera or contacting process whereby various images are made thinner without changing shape or position. The image area remains essentially the same except for a narrow reduction around its perimeter. Alternative term: *skinny*.

coating—(1) An unbroken, clear film applied to a substrate in layers to protect and seal it, or to make it glossy. (2) Applying waxes, adhesives, varnishes, or other protective or sealable chemicals to a substrate during the converting process. (3) The mineral substances (clay, blanc fixe, satin white, etc.) applied to the surface of a paper or board. (4) In photography and photomechanics, applying varnishes and other mixtures to plates and negatives; or applying light-sensitive solutions to plates or film.

color bar—A device printed in a trim area of a press sheet to monitor printing variables, such as trapping, ink density, dot gain, and print contrast. It usually consists of overprints of two- and three-color solids and tints; solid and tint blocks of cyan, magenta, yellow, and black; and additional aids, such as resolution targets and dot gain scales. Alternative terms: *color control strip; color control bar*.

color correction—Photographic, electronic, or manual procedure used to compensate for the deficiencies of the process inks and color separation.

color electronic prepress system (CEPS)—A computer-based image manipulation and page-makeup system for graphic arts applications. These systems produce, at very high speed, complete sets of separations to single- or double-page size, with all illustrations, tints, and rules in their correct locations. Some systems also integrate text.

color separation—Using red, green, and blue filters to divide the colors of a multicolored original into the three process colors and black. The four resulting film intermediates are used to prepare the yellow, magenta, cyan, and black printing plates. Color separation is most often accomplished with an electronic color scanner, but film-contacting and process-camera methods are also employed on occasion.

color strength—(1) The relative amounts of pigment in an ink film. (2) The concentration or dilution of a color. See *saturation*.

common-impression press—A flexo, or sheetfed or web offset, press with one large impression cylinder, which holds or supports the substrate, and several color stations around it.

common-impression cylinder (CIC)—A large cylinder that holds or supports the substrate and has several color stations positioned around it. On some web and sheetfed offset presses, the common-impression cylinder is in contact with several blanket cylinders. This configuration is used to print multicolor work on one side of the web or sheet.

complementary flats—A set of two or more pin-registered film flats, each of which carries different image elements for one particular printing color. During platemaking, the complementary flats are exposed sequentially to the same printing plate.

composite—A single film carrying two or more images (usually line, halftone, or screen tint) as a result of photocombining (contacting) two or more separate film images or film flats.

comprehensive—A precise layout, prepared by the graphic designer, that shows the final position of all type and illustrations. Also called *comp* and *mock-up*.

contact photography—A photographic process used to reproduce images by exposing a light-sensitive material through a transparent or translucent (transmission) original placed over it in a vacuum frame.

continuous tone—A photographic image or art (such as a wash drawing) that has infinite tone gradations between the lightest highlights and the deepest shadows.

cover paper—Paper used to protect a document and represent it appropriately. They are available coated, in white and numerous colors, and in different finishes, grades, and basis weights.

crop marks—Small lines placed in the margin or on an overlay, denoting the image areas to be reproduced.

CRT—Cathode-ray tube.

curl—Uneven warping of the edges of a sheet aggravated by moisture and affected by the direction of the paper fibers.

cylinder press—(1) Printing equipment in which the type form is held on a reciprocating flatbed that moves alternately under the inking rollers and a large rotating cylinder. The cylinder carries the paper sheet, pressing it against the type form. (2) A screen printing press in which the substrate, wrapped around a rotating drum, contacts the printing surface of a moving screen and is discharged onto a conveyor after printing. (3) A press used for diecutting.

D

dampening system—A series of rollers that moisten the printing plate with a metered flow of a water-based solution containing such additives as acid, gum arabic, and isopropyl alcohol, or other wetting agents.

dancer roller—A weighted or spring-tensioned controlled roller positioned between a paper roll and a press unit on a web press. It detects and removes web slack by controlling the paper reel brake.

dandy roll—The hollow, wire-covered cylinder on a papermaking machine that improves paper formation or presses a watermark into the wet, newly formed web.

delivery—(1) The section of a printing press that receives, jogs, and stacks the printed sheet. (2) The output end of bindery equipment.

descender—The portion of a lowercase type character that extends below the common baseline of a typeface design, such as in "g," "j," "p," "q," and "y."

desktop publishing—A compact publishing system that includes a personal computer (usually with a color monitor); word processing, page-makeup, illustration, and other software; digitized type fonts; a laser printer; and other peripherals, such as an optical image scanner. It is used mostly to produce low-volume, low-resolution work. More sophisticated software and systems can yield higher quality artwork and text, which can be merged and output as color-separated, registered film on an imagesetter.

die—(1) A pattern of sharp knives or metal tools used to stamp, cut, or emboss specific shapes, designs, and letters into a substrate. (2) A plate cut, etched, or embossed in intaglio to provide a raised impression on paper.

diecutting—Using sharp steel rules to slice paper or board to a specific shape on a printing press or a special stamping press.

diffusion transfer—A process used to produce positive screened prints and line prints on paper, film, or lithographic plates by physically transferring the image during processing from an exposed special light-sensitive material (a negative sheet with a silver emulsion) to a sheet of paper, film, or aluminum (the receiver sheet).

digester—A large tank in which wood chips are cooked to remove lignin from them in the chemical pulping process.

digital halftone—A halftone produced with a scanner, or video digitizer, computer system, and imagesetter as opposed to a conventional halftone made with a contact halftone screen and a process camera.

dimensional stability—How well a sheet of paper resists dimensional change when its moisture content is altered.

direct digital color proof—A prepress color proof that is imaged directly from digital data without the intermediate steps of film and contact exposure.

direct stencil—A light-sensitive liquid emulsion that is squeegeed into a screen printing fabric, dried, exposed in contact to a positive, and developed to form an outline (stencil) image after processing.

display type—Those type styles and sizes designed mainly for use as headline and advertising matter, instead of as straight text or body composition. Alternative term: *display matter*.

doctor blade—(1) A steel blade that wipes the excess (surface) ink or coating from a cylinder before printing. (2) A steel or wooden blade used to keep cylinder surfaces clean and free from paper, pulp, size, or other material during papermaking.

drop-on-demand (DOD) ink jet—A nonimpact printing method in which ink droplets are emitted only when required for imaging. Also known as *asynchronous ink jet*.

DTP—Desktop publishing. Also called *electronic publishing*.

duotone—A special effects technique of making a two-color halftone reproduction from a single-color original. In the most common type of duotone, the two halftones are printed in two different colors.

E

electrography, or ionography—A nonimpact printing technique in which paper with a conductive base layer is coated with a nonconductive thermoplastic material. A set of electrode styli apply an electric charge to areas of the substrate corresponding to the latent image of the original. Following the charging step, the paper is imaged by a toner system similar to that used in electrostatic copying devices.

electronic publishing—Any system using a computer and related word processing and design and page-makeup software to create paginated text and graphics. The text and graphics are output to a laser printer with a PostScript interpreter and/or imagesetter at varying degrees of resolution from a minimum of 300 dots per inch to maximums exceeding 1,250 dots per inch. See also *desktop publishing*.

electrophotography—Processes (including xerography and laser printing) that produce images by passing toner particles over an intermediate photoconductor drum, which receives an electrical charge that enables it to transfer and fuse the toner particles to plain (untreated) paper, forming the image.

electrostatic plate—An organic photoconductor that serves as an offset lithographic image carrier.

electrotype—A duplicate relief printing plate that is made by molding a sheet of hot plastic or wax against the original relief plate, electroplating the mold with a coating of copper or nickel, shaping the plate into a cylinder, and backing it with a plastic, wood, or metal support material.

embossing—(1) Using raised dies to print text or designs in relief on any one of a variety of paper stocks. (2) The swelling of a lithographic offset blanket caused by ink solvent absorption. Alternative term: *blanket embossing*. (3) Undesirable condition resulting from heavy ink coverage in solid image areas on a press sheet. The ink pulls away from the paper as it is peeled from the blanket following impression, causing the solid image areas to appear as high relief images. Also called *waffling*.

emulsion—Photographic term for a gelatin or colloidal solution holding light-sensitive salts of silver in suspension. It is used as the light-sensitive coating on photographic film or plates in photomechanical printing processes.

F

fake color—Varied color areas created using flat colors. Depending on the number of different colors printed, the illustration can approach the appearance of full-color reproduction.

feeder—(1) A mechanism that separates, lifts, and passes individual press sheets from the top of a pile table onto the feedboard to front stops. The sheets are laterally positioned on the feedboard by a side guide and then fed into the first printing unit. Alternative terms: *feeding head; stream feeder*. (2) The device that forwards signatures or newspaper inserts, etc., through an in-line finishing system.

felt side—The top side of the paper formed on the paper machine wire. It is the preferred side for printing. It is the opposite of the wire side.

fiber—Wood particles used in the papermaking process.

fillers—(1) Inorganic materials, like titanium dioxide and other white pigments, that are added to the paper furnish to improve opacity and brightness. (2) Inert substance used in a composition to increase bulk and strength, and possibly lower the cost.

film image assembly—Positioning, mounting, and securing various individual films to one carrier sheet in preparation for platemaking. Also called *stripping*.

finishing—Graphic arts production procedures that are performed after press operations, including folding, trimming, assembling, diecutting, and foil stamping.

flat—(1) A sheet of plastic or goldenrod paper to which negatives or positives have been attached (stripped) for exposure as a unit onto a printing plate. (2) Lacking contrast, color, or brilliance.

flat color—An ink specially formulated to produce a desired hue, printed as a solid, tint, or halftone. Flat color inks are not designed to be overprinted with other inks, as process-color inks are. The term may also be used to refer to an image that only contains color at a uniform density in any one segment.

flatbed press—A printing press in which the form is held in a horizontal platen.

flatbed scanner—A scanner on which the original is placed on a horizontal table instead of a rotary drum.

flexography—A method of rotary relief printing characterized by the use of flexible rubber, or plastic, plates with raised image areas and fluid, rapid-drying inks.

flood coat—In screen printing, an even coating of ink, which covers the surface of the screen, but is not forced through the image areas. This ensures that the entire screen receives the proper ink supply during impression.

flush left—Lines of type composition aligned to the left margin, with a ragged right margin. See *justification*.

flush right—Lines of composition aligned to the right margin with a ragged left margin. See *justification.*

flying paster—An automatic device that splices a new roll of paper to an expiring roll while the expiring roll is still moving at full press speed.

folder—A machine that bends and creases printed sheets of paper to particular specifications during binding and finishing.

folio—In printing, a page number, often placed at the outside of the running head, at the top (head) of the page. See also *header, running head.*

footer—A book's title or a chapter title printed at the bottom of a page. A drop folio (page number) may or may not be included.

fountain roller—A metal roller that rotates intermittently or continuously in the ink or dampening fountain and carries the ink or dampening solution on its metal surface.

fourdrinier machine—Paper machine that forms a continuous web of paper on a horizontal, forward-moving, endless wire belt.

furnish—The mixture of fibrous and nonfibrous materials like fillers, sizing, and colorants in a water suspension from which paper or paperboard is made.

G

galley—(1) Phototypesetter output, usually in single columns of type on long sheets of photographic paper, which serves as preliminary proofs. (2) The final typeset (or imageset) copy output to photographic paper, or film. (3) A long, shallow tray used to store and proof handset type.

gloss—The relative amount of incident light reflected from a surface. Papers are said to have varying degrees of gloss.

grain direction—In papermaking, the alignment of fibers in the direction of web travel. Terms like across the grain, which is at right angles to or opposite the paper grain direction, and against the grain, which is at right angles to the paper grain in the direction of the sheet's fibers, are also used.

grain-long—A paper grain direction that parallels the long dimension of the sheet.

grain-short—A paper grain direction that parallels the short dimension of the sheet.

grammage—The weight in grams of a single sheet of paper with an area of one square meter.

gravure—An intaglio printing process in which minute depressions, sometimes called cells, that form the image are engraved or etched below the nonimage area in the surface of the printing cylinder. The cylinder is immersed in ink, and the excess ink is scraped off by a blade. When paper or another substrate comes in contact with the printing cylinder, ink is transferred.

gravure cylinder—The image carrier in gravure printing.

gray balance—The dot values for yellow, magenta, and cyan that produce a neutral gray when printed at a normal density.

gray component replacement (GCR)—An electronic color scanning capability in which values of yellow, magenta, and cyan forming a neutral gray are replaced with an appropriate value of black.

grayness—An attribute calculated from density readings that relates to the degree of three-color contamination in a cyan, magenta, or yellow process-color ink. As grayness values increase, an ink exhibits lower saturation or purity.

gray scale—A reflection or transmission strip showing neutral tones in a range of graduated steps. It is exposed alongside originals during photography and used to time development, determine color balance, or measure density range, tone reproduction, and print contrast. Gray scales can also be used to check focus and resolution.

gripper—(1) A metal clamp that grasps and holds a sheet in position as it travels through a sheetfed press. (2) The reference edge of a layout, film flat, or printing plate that corresponds to the sheet edge held by the grippers on the press.

H

halftone—A printed reproduction of a continuous-tone image composed of dots that vary in frequency (number per square inch), size, or density, producing tonal gradations. The term is also applied to the process and plates used to produce this image.

halftone screen—A device placed in front of high-contrast photosensitive material and through which exposures of continuous-tone copy are made to produce an image pattern of small, solid dots (or narrow lines) varying in size (or width) to represent varying tone values. A contact screen (which is placed in contact with the photosensitive material) is a sheet of film having a pattern of varying densities: most commonly vignetted dots.

hardware—The electric, electronic, magnetic, and mechanical components of a computer system.

header—A book's title or a chapter title printed at the top of a page and often with a folio (page number). Alternative term: running head. See *folio, footer.*

heatset press—A web offset press that includes a hot-air dryer and chill rolls.

highlight—The lightest or whitest area of an original or reproduction, represented by the densest portion of a continuous-tone negative and by the smallest dot formation on a halftone and printing plate.

hot-air dryer—A dryer on a web offset press that uses hot air to remove most of the solvents from the printed ink film.

hue—The name of a color; e.g., red, green, blue, or some combination term, such as bluish green.

I

imagesetter—A device used to output fully paginated text and graphic images at a high resolution onto photographic film, paper, or plates.

impression cylinder—The large-diameter roller on a lithographic printing press that provides the pressure needed to transfer ink to paper.

indirect, or transfer, stencil systems—A method of creating a stencil for screen printing by exposing the stencil film to a film positive, processing the exposed stencil film, and adhering it to the printing screen.

infeed—(1) The section of a sheetfed press where the sheet is transferred from the registering devices of the feedboard to the first impression cylinder. (2) The set of rollers controlling web tension ahead of the first unit on a web press.

inking system—The section of a printing press that distributes ink to the plate.

in-line press—A nonperfecting press with one or more printing units, each consisting of an inking system, a dampening system, a plate cylinder, a blanket cylinder, and an impression cylinder.

J

justification—The process of composing a line of type by spacing between the words and characters to fill an exact measure, thus aligning the type at both margins.

K

kerning—The process of reducing the letterspacing between certain letter combinations (e.g., a capital "A" and a capital "V") to achieve aesthetically pleasing results.

knife-cut stencil—A screen printing stencil cut from film and adhered to the underside of the screen.

knockout, or reverse—Type that appears as white on a black or dark-colored background. Also called a *dropout*.

L

lap register, or trap—Overlapping two colors at their junction to improve image fit and lessen image distortion on the press.

laser—A high-energy, coherent (single-wavelength) light source. The small spot of light produced by the laser makes it possible to expose light-sensitive and photoconductive materials at high speed and high resolution.

latex-treated papers—Papers that have their fibrous network impregnated with latex for durability, high-edge tear resistance, wet strength, flexibility, and leatherlike properties.

layout—(1) A guide prepared to show the arrangement and location of all the type, illustrations, and line art that are combined together to compose the film flat. (2) One of three levels of concepts—thumbnails, roughs, and comprehensive—that the designer uses to render the appearance of the finished job.

leading—The amount of space between the baseline of one line of type and the baseline of the adjacent line. This distance is usually greater than the type size.

ledger papers—Papers made from all chemical wood pulp from a combination of wood and cotton fibers, or from 100% cotton fiber, in heavier basis weights than bond papers.

letterpress—The method of printing in which the image, or ink-bearing areas, of the printing plate are in relief, i.e., raised above the nonimage areas.

letterspace—To add space between the characters of a word or group of words, either for emphasis or for aesthetic purposes when justifying text.

ligature—Two or more characters that are specially modified in design to be cast or exposed together as one unit, frequently with connecting strokes. Some examples include fi, ff, ffi, fl, and ffl.

lightweight printing papers—Paper with a basic size of 25×38 in. weighing in the range of 17–40 lbs./ream (25–59 g/m²).

lignin—A glue-like substance that holds wood fibers together. It is removed from the wood when making pulp.

line copy—Type matter and drawings that can be reproduced without the use of a halftone screen.

line gauge—A ruler scaled in picas and points for a typographer's use. Line gauges come in different sizes, materials, and configurations and may include other scales, such as inches, agate lines, etc.

line spacing—See *leading*.

liquid inks—Fluid inks like flexographic and gravure inks.

lithography—A printing process in which the image carrier is chemically treated so that the nonimage areas are receptive to water (i.e., dampening or fountain solution) and repel ink while the image areas are receptive to ink and repel water. The image carrier is said to be planographic, or flat and smooth.

lowercase—The uncapitalized letters of the alphabet. Originally called lowercase because the lead type version was located in the lower portion of the type case.

M

magnetography—See *nonimpact printer*.

manifold paper—A very thin paper, frequently used as carbon paper in multipart forms.

markup—The process of indicating the typographic specifications for a job, including typestyle and size, format and spacing, and sometimes machine codes, directly on the manuscript, to guide the typesetter.

mask—(1) A photographic negative or positive that is placed over a color transparency or individual separation to selectively increase total density. Masks are used to reduce the tonal scale, improve highlight or shadow detail, and correct color excesses or deficiencies. The process itself is referred to as masking. (2) A sheet placed over or around printing detail to prevent the passage of actinic light during exposure. (3) A pasteup overlay that indicates the placement of art requiring special handling. (4) A thin sheet used to secure the white margins on a photograph.

mechanical—The assembly of all page elements, including text and line art, properly proportioned and positioned, in camera-ready form. Also called *pasteup.*

middletones—The range of tonal values between the highlight and shadow areas. Alternative term: *midtone.*

modem—A device that serves as an interface, or communications link, between one computer workstation and another, or a network of computers. Electronic information can then be transferred between workstations or among network participants over conventional telephone lines.

moiré—An undesirable, unintended interference pattern caused by the out-of-register overlap of two or more regular patterns, such as dots or lines. In process-color printing, screen angles are selected to minimize this pattern. If the angles are not correct, an objectionable effect may be produced.

monitor screen—A cathode-ray tube device on which image information is displayed in conjunction with a workstation.

monofilament mesh—A screen printing image carrier mesh that consists of single strands of synthetic fiber woven together to form a porous material.

mouse—A hand-held device that controls the menu and moves the cursor on a computer screen.

multifilament mesh—A screen printing image carrier mesh that consists of many fine threads twisted together to form a single thread. These threads are woven together to form the mesh.

N

negative-working plate—A printing plate exposed through a film negative. Areas exposed to light become the image areas.

news ink—An ink specially designed for use on newsprint. Consisting basically of carbon black or colored pigments dispersed in mineral oil vehicles, news inks dry by absorption.

newsprint—Paper manufactured mostly from groundwood or mechanical pulp specifically for newspaper printing. It has a basis weight of 25–32 pounds for a basic size of 24×36 in.

nonimpact printer—A printing device that creates letters or images on a substrate without striking it. Photocopiers, laser printers, and ink jet printers are some examples.

nonperfecting—A press that does not print on both sides of the substrate in a single pass.

O

OCR—Optical character recognition.

offset blanket—A fabric coated with synthetic rubber that transfers the image from the printing plate to the substrate. It is carried by the blanket cylinder.

offset printing—An indirect printing method in which the inked image on a press plate is first transferred to a rubber blanket that in turn "offsets" the inked impression to a press sheet.

onionskin—A lightweight, air-dried, cockle-finish bond paper.

opacity—The degree to which light will not pass through a substrate or ink.

opaque—(1) Any material that will not permit the passage of light. (2) In film assembly a nontransparent pigment (usually red or black) applied to pinholes or other areas of film negatives to prevent light from passing through during platemaking.

optical character recognition (OCR)—A technique in which any printed, typed, or handwritten copy or graphic images are scanned by an electronic reader that converts them into a form that can be read, interpreted, and displayed by computers.

outfeed and rewind section—The area at the end of a flexo press that moves the substrate (either sheets or rolls) out of the press and, in the case of rolls, rewinds the web.

overlay—A sheet of translucent or transparent tissue, acetate, or polyester attached over the face of the primary artwork (paste-up) and used to indicate surprints, knockouts, overlapping or butting flat colors, placement of alternate or additional copy, or previously separated color art.

overlay proof—Thin, transparent pigmented or dyed sheets of plastic film that are registered to each other in a specific order and taped or pin-registered to a base sheet. Each film carries the printed image for a different process color, which, when combined, creates a composite simulating the final printed piece.

P

paint program—A graphics-oriented computer program that creates bit-mapped art. Electronic airbrushing and pixel-level editing are two features of paint programs.

paper additives—Nonfibrous substances—fillers and dyes—that are added during papermaking to alter a paper's properties.

paperback—A book with a flexible paper binding.

paperboard—A paper product with a greater basis weight, thickness, and rigidity than paper. With a few exceptions, paperboard has a thickness of 12 points (0.3 mm) or more. Also called *cardboard*.

parchment—A fine, translucent paper made from the tanned hide of a sheep or goat.

paste inks—Inks that are nonfluid. Lithographic, letterpress, screen printing, and some news inks are paste inks.

pasteup—The camera-ready assembly of type and line art (e.g., drawings) prepared manually or electronically for photographic reproduction. Also called *mechanical* and *photomechanical.*

perfecting—Printing both sides of a sheet in the same pass through the press.

photocombining—The process of assembling illustrations that fit closely to (or butt) other illustrations on complementary flats and then contacting them onto a single film before platemaking.

photocomposing—Exposing multiple images to a plate from a single film. Alternative term: *step-and-repeat.*

photodirect plates—A type of lithographic plate that can be produced directly in either camera or projection types of equipment. The intermediate step of making a photographic negative or positive has been eliminated.

photopolymer—A plastic designed so that it changes upon exposure to light. Photopolymer films and plates are used in printing. Photopolymer plates are used most often in flexography.

photostencils—Screen printing stencils composed of a light-sensitive coating or emulsion that hardens when exposed to an ultraviolet light source.

phototypesetting—The act of composing type and reproducing it on photographic film or paper.

pica—A printer's unit of linear measure, equal to approximately one-sixth of an inch. There are twelve points in a pica and approximately six picas in an inch.

pick resistance—How well a paper surface resists force before splitting or rupturing.

picking—The delamination, splitting, or tearing of paper surface fibers that occurs when the tack of the ink exceeds the surface strength of the paper.

pigment—Fine, solid particles derived from natural or synthetic sources and used to impart colors to inks. They have varying degrees of resistance to water, alcohol, and other chemicals and are generally insoluble in the ink vehicle.

pinhole—A small, unwanted, transparent area in the developed emulsion of a negative or positive. It is usually caused by dust or other defects on the copy, copyboard glass, or film.

pixel—Picture element. The smallest tonal element in a digital imaging or display system.

plate cylinder—In lithography, the cylinder that holds the printing plate tightly and in register on press. It allows the plate to be contacted by the dampening rollers, which wet the nonimage area, and the inking rollers, which ink the image area, then transfers the inked image to the blanket.

platemaking—Preparing a printing plate or other image carrier from a film or flat, including sensitizing the surface if the plate was not presensitized by the manufacturer, exposing it through the flat, and developing or processing and finishing it so that it is ready for the press.

platen press—A printing press with a flat printing surface and a flat impression surface.

point size—The height of the body of a typeface in units of linear measure equal to 0.0138 in. Also called *type size*.

positive-working plate—An image carrier that is exposed through a film positive. Plate areas exposed to light become the nonimage areas after processing.

posterizations—A special effects photographic technique that renders continuous-tone copy into an image represented by a few broad, flat, dark middletones and shadow areas. All highlight and light middletone areas are eliminated.

prepress—All printing operations prior to presswork, including design and layout, typesetting/imagesetting, graphic arts photography, color separation, image assembly, and platemaking.

prepress proofing—Producing a simulation of the final printed piece by various methods, such as photochemical methods (e.g., an overlay of dye or pigment images on transparent film base), instead of photomechanical methods (ink on paper). Also called *offpress proofing*.

presensitized plate—A sheet of metal or paper supplied to the user with the light-sensitive material already coated on the surface and ready for exposure to a negative or positive.

press—The machine that creates the final printed image.

press section—In a papermaking machine, the area where water is removed from the web by suction and applied pressure.

printability—The combination of print quality characteristics that enhance the reproduction of an original in any printing process.

printer—(1) Any computer output device that produces results in readable form on paper. (2) Color-separated halftone films that will transfer the characteristics of each specific process color in a given job to the corresponding printing plate prior to presswork. (3) The person or company that operates printing presses.

printer's spread—A pair of pages placed across a fold from each other in printing. See *reader's spread*.

printing section—One of the four sections on a typical flexographic press. It comes after the unwind or infeed section and before the drying section. Each printing unit on a single- or multicolor press has an inking system, a plate cylinder, and an impression cylinder.

printing unit—The sections on printing presses that house the components for reproducing an image on the substrate. In lithography, a printing unit includes the inking and dampening systems and the plate, blanket, and impression cylinders.

process colors—The three subtractive primary colors used in photomechanical printing (cyan, magenta, yellow) plus black.

processing—Chemically treating photographic papers, films, and plates after exposure.

proof—A prototype of the printed job made photomechanically from plates (a press proof), photochemically from film and dyes, or digitally from electronic data (prepress proofs). Prepress proofs serve as samples for the customer and guides for the press operators. Press proofs are approved by the customer and/or plant supervisor before the actual pressrun.

proof scan—A low-resolution scan that allows the operator to check the position and quality of the scan.

proofing—Producing simulated versions of the final reproduction from films and dyes or digitized data (prepress proofing) or producing trial images directly from the plate (press proofing).

pulp—The substance produced mechanically or chemically from fibrous cellulose raw materials for use in papermaking.

Q

quad left—A command code in a phototypesetter that instructs the machine to position all text to the left side of the line. A minimum of interword spacing and letterspacing is used in the portion of the line containing characters. The right portion contains only space. Also known as *flush left*.

R

ragged right—Type that is not flush right. All lines end in a different column, giving the right margin a ragged appearance.

reader's spread—A pair of pages that are across the gutter from each other *after the book is assembled*. See also *printer's spread*.

ream—500 sheets of paper.

reducer—(1) An additive that softens printing ink and reduces its tack. (2) Chemical that reduces the density of a photographic image by removing silver.

reflectance—Ratio between the amount of light reflected from a given tone area and the amount reflected from a white area.

reflection copy—A photographic print, painting, or other opaque copy used as original art for reproduction. Such copy is viewed by the light reflected from its surface and can only be photoreproduced with front illumination (as from a graphic arts camera) as opposed to the backlighting used to view and reproduce transmission copy (i.e., slides and transparencies).

register marks—Small reference patterns, guides, or crosses placed on originals before reproduction to aid in color separation and positioning negatives for stripping. They are also placed along the margins of film flats to aid in color registration and correct alignment of overprinted colors on press sheets.

relative humidity—The amount of moisture present in the air, expressed as a percentage of the amount of moisture required to saturate the air at a given temperature.

relief printing—A printing process using an image carrier on which the image areas are raised above the nonimage areas.

reverse, or knockout—Type that appears as white on a black or dark colored background. Also known as a *dropout*.

rider roller—A rigid, friction-driven roller in the press inking system that helps to break down, distribute, and transfer the ink while remaining in contact with one or more resilient rollers.

roll sheeter—Device that cuts a roll or web of paper into sheets and sends them to the feeder on a sheetfed press. See *sheeter*.

roll-to-roll printing—Printing webs of substrates and then rewinding them directly onto another roll core after printing.

rotary press—Any printing press in which the printing plate or surface is cylindrical and rotates and prints continuously, usually at high speed, on both web and sheetfed stocks.

rotogravure—A printing process that uses an engraved or etched cylinder as an image carrier. Image areas are etched or engraved below nonimage areas in the form of tiny sunken cells. The cylinder is immersed in ink, and the excess ink is scraped off by a blade. When the substrate contacts the printing cylinder, ink transfers, forming the image.

rough—A crude or basic sketch of a layout, design, drawing, etc.

run-of-press (ROP) color—Usually describes the "standard" ink colors for a given pressrun.

running head—Information that appears at the top of every page or many pages of a document, such as chapter titles and book titles. See also *footer*.

S

saddle stitching—A binding in which wire stitches that resemble staples pass through the centerfold of one or more folded signatures. When being stitched, signatures are placed over a saddle-like device. Alternative term: *wire stitching*.

safety paper—Paper produced with special chemicals and mechanical properties that make it easier to expose forgery or any alterations of checks and other negotiable, legal documents.

sans serif—Typeface designs, such as Helvetica, that lack the small extensions on the ascenders and descenders called *serifs*.

saturation—(1) The degree to which a chromatic color differs from a gray of the same brightness. In other words, how a color varies from pastel (low saturation) to pure (high saturation). In the Munsell system, this is called chroma. (2) The quality of visual perception that permits a judgment of different purities of any one dominant wavelength.

scanner—An electromechanical device that converts an image such as artwork or a photograph, into its electronic equivalent for subsequent computer storage, manipulation, and output.

screen printing—A printing process in which a squeegee forces ink through a porous mesh image carrier, or screen, covered by a stencil that blocks the nonimage areas. Ink pressed through the open image areas of the screen forms the image on the substrate.

screen tints—A halftone film with a uniform dot size throughout. It is rated by its approximate printing dot size value, such as 20%, 50%, etc.

scuff resistance—A dried ink film's ability to withstand scuffing.

serif—The short, usually perpendicular line found at the end of the unconnected or finishing stroke of a character. Serifs may vary in weight, length, and shape, and contribute greatly to the style of the typeface.

shadow—The darker or denser areas of an original, film positive, or halftone reproduction.

sheeter—(1) A device on a printing press that converts continuous forms into smaller sheets. (2) A specific web press delivery unit that cuts the printed web into individual sheets. (3) A separate device used in screen printing to cut cloth or other substrates into sheets. See *roll sheeter.*

sheetfed press—A printing press that feeds and prints on individual sheets of paper (or another substrate). Some sheetfed presses employ a rollfed system in which rolls of paper are cut into sheets before they enter the feeder; however, most sheetfed presses forward individual sheets directly to the feeder.

shortening compounds—Ink additives that shorten an ink and reduce its tendency to fly or mist.

show-through—A term used to describe the visibility of printed material from the opposite side of the sheet. This characteristic is proportional to the transparency of the substrate and the oiliness of the ink.

slip compound—An ink additive that improves the scuff resistance of a printed ink film.

softcover—See *paperback*.

software—The stored instructions (programs) that initiate the various functions of a computer (hardware). Instructions may be written in machine language or in another programming language, then compiled, interpreted, or assembled into machine language. Word processing, page layout, and drawing programs are a few of the software programs used in the graphic arts. There are also other more specialized software programs that control high-end color electronic prepress systems and even some presswork applications.

solvent—(1) A material, usually a liquid, capable of dissolving another substance, usually a solid, to form a solution. (2) A component of the vehicle in printing inks that disperses the pigment and keeps the solid binder liquid enough for use in the printing process.

specifications—A detailed description of the requirements for a job, the typography in particular. Also called *speccing*.

specimen book—(1) A catalog illustrating the variety and range of typefaces available from a particular company, including fonts, point sizes, sorts, rules, ornaments, etc. (2) Printed samples of standard ink colors provided by the ink manufacturer, usually as solid color blocks and sometimes with percentage tints or halftone illustrations.

splice—The area where two rolls are joined to form a continuous roll. The splice can be made while the press is running at full speed by using an automatic splicing device, either a flying paster or a zero-speed splicer.

spot color printing—The selective addition of a non-process-color ink to a printing job.

spread—(1) A line image with edges that have been moved slightly outward to allow a color or tint to overlap. (2) Two facing pages in a book or magazine. Also called a *reader's spread*.

squeegee—(1) A rubber or plastic blade used to force ink through the open areas of a screen-printing stencil and mesh to form an image on the substrate. (2) A blade used to sweep solution from printing plates during manual processing.

stack press—A flexo press that has all of its individual color stations vertically stacked one over another.

stem—The primary vertical stroke of a type character.

step-and-repeat—Exposing multiple images onto a single film or a single printing plate from a single negative or positive flat. Special step-and-repeat contact frames, projection platemakers, and imposing cameras are used to automate this process.

stereotype—A duplicate relief printing plate made by casting a lead alloy into a paper mold of the original plate.

stiffening agents—Ink additives that stiffen an ink that is too liquid and fails to print cleanly and sharply.

stripping—The act of combining and positioning all of the image elements from all of the film negatives or positives together as a single unit for platemaking. Also known as *image assembly*.

substrate—Any base material with a surface that can be printed or coated.

subtractive color process—A means of producing a color reproduction or image with combinations of yellow, magenta, and cyan colorants on a white substrate.

supercalendering—A method of producing a very high gloss surface on paper stock by passing the sheet between a series of heated metal rollers under pressure.

surface plate—A lithographic plate in which the light-sensitive coating becomes the printing image. Surface plates can be either presensitized or wipe-on.

surface strength—The ability of a paper to resist a perpendicularly applied force, such as that in the splitting of an ink film, to its surface before picking or rupturing occurs.

T

tack—The cohesion between ink particles, measured by gauging the force required to split an ink film between two surfaces.

template—In electronic publishing, a guide for a standard document design or format, i.e., a page layout guide for a textbook.

tensile strength—The amount of stress needed to break paper by pulling it.

text paper—Paper with a textured surface. It has wove, antique, vellum, and felt types of finishes, which may have light, medium, or heavy pattern depths that are either produced on either paper machine, or embossed after papermaking.

thumbnail sketch—Crude, small pencil drawings used to develop the initial concept for a design.

tint—An image element with an even shading produced by either a halftone dot screen of various shapes and sizes, or fine parallel lines.

toner—(1) A high-strength pigment or ink. (2) The electrostatically charged carbon particles suspended in a liquid solvent that form the printed image when fused to the substrate with heat during xerography.

transmission copy—A slide or transparency used as original art for reproduction. Such copy is viewed by the light transmitted through its surface and can only be photoreproduced with back illumination.

transmittance—Fraction of transmitted incident light that passes through a tone area without being absorbed or scattered.

trap, or lap register—The overlapping of a narrow strip—the lap—of one color over another at their juncture to make it easier to fit the colors together on the press.

trapping, ink—The ability of a printed ink film to accept ink from the press. If the first-down ink has dried, the process is called *dry trapping*. If the print is still wet, it is called *wet trapping*. In printing on multicolor presses, wet trapping is of great importance in controlling color.

type family—A set of typefaces derived from one basic design, e.g., bold, italic, and condensed variations of the original face.

typeface—A distinctive type design, usually produced in a range of sizes (fonts) and variations, including **bold** and *italic*.

typography—The art and craft of creating and/or setting type.

U

ultraviolet (UV) inks—Printing inks containing an activator that causes the polymerization of binders and solvents after exposure to a source of ultraviolet radiation.

undercolor removal (UCR)—A technique used to reduce the yellow, magenta, and cyan dot percentages in neutral dark tones by replacing them with increased amounts of black ink.

unsharp masking (USM)—The increase of tonal contrast where light and dark tones come together at the edges of the images.

unwind section—The first section of flexographic and roto-gravure presses.

uppercase—The capitalized letters of the alphabet and other symbols produced when the "shift" key on a typewriter-style keyboard is depressed.

V

vacuum frame—A device that holds film or plates in place by withdrawing air through small holes in a supporting surface. Also called *contact printing frame; vacuum back*.

varnish—(1) A thin protective coating applied to a printed sheet to protect the image and improve appearance. (2) The major component of an ink vehicle, consisting of solvent plus a resin or drying oil.

vehicle—The liquid component of a printing ink.

vignette—(1) A halftone, drawing, or engraved illustration in which the background gradually fades away from the principal subject until it finally blends into the nonimage areas of the print. (2) An image segment with densities varying from highlight to white. (3) Any small decorative illustration or design used to ornament a book, periodical, or other printed matter, especially before the title page and at the ends of chapters.

vignetted dots—Dots that gradually vary in density from center to edges.

viscosity—A measure of how well a printing ink, glue, or other fluid resists flowing. Viscosity is the opposite of fluidity.

W

water-repellent—Repels water. The nonimage area of a lithographic plate is water-repellent or hydrophobic.

wax—An ink additive that improves slip and resistance, prevents setoff, and reduces tack.

web offset—A lithographic printing process in which a press prints on a continuous roll of paper instead of individual sheets.

web press—A rotary press that prints on a continuous web, or ribbon, of paper fed from a roll and threaded through the press.

wedding paper—A fancy paper with a very uniform, closed formation and a refined surface lacking glare.

wetting agent—Any of various chemical substances that reduce the surface tension of a liquid, thereby promoting smoother and more uniform results.

window method—A procedure in which a sized adhesive-backed masking material is placed on the pasteup board where halftones or separate artwork will print. When photographed, the mask produces a clear area on the negative into which the halftone or artwork is stripped during image assembly.

wipe-on plate—Lithographic plate on which a light-sensitive coating is wiped on, or applied manually or by machine.

wire side—The side of a sheet of paper that was formed in contact with the wire of the paper machine during manufacturing.

work-and-tumble—A printing imposition where a single printing plate contains all of the pages or images to be printed on both sides of the press sheet with a single color of ink. The first side of the sheet is printed, the sheet is flopped end for end, the second side is printed, and then the sheet is cut in half (parallel to its ends) to yield two identical units.

work-and-turn—A printing imposition where a single printing plate contains all of the pages or images to be printed on both sides of the press sheet with a single color of ink. The first side of the sheet is printed, the sheet is turned over sideways from left to right, the second side is printed, and then the sheet is cut in half (parallel to the sides) to yield two identical sides.

X

xerography—An electrostatic, nonimpact printing process in which heat fuses dry ink toner particles to electrically charged areas of the substrate, forming a permanent image. The charged areas of the substrate appear dark on the reproduction, while the uncharged areas remain white.

x-height—A term used to describe the body height of a type character. It is expressed as the total character height without ascenders or descenders. The letters "x" and "z" from each typeface are selected to serve as examples of the face body height because they rest on the baseline and vary less in height than curved letters. Also called *z-height*.

Index

Additive color reproduction process   66–70
Adhesive binding   176–177
Art, continuous tone   36
  line   32–36
  scaling   37
Assembling   174
Automatic cylinder press   147–148
Automatic flatbed press   147–148

Back gluing   182
Backing   180–182
Backlining   182
Basic size   198
Basis weight   198
Bezier curves   55
Bimetal plates   111
Binding,   174–186
  adhesive   176–177
  case   179–183
  comb   184
  loose-leaf   183
  mechanical   183–185
  perfect   176–177
  spiral   184
  wire stitching   174–176
Blanks   201
Bond papers   201–202
Box tools   52
Brightness   71
Bristol papers   202
Brush-and-ink line art   32–33
Buckle folder   169–170
Building-in   183

Caliper   199
Camera-ready copy   31
Carbonless papers   202

Case binding,   179–183
  covering process   182–183
  edition binding   179
  job binding   179–180
  library binding   179–180
  precovering operations   180
Casing-in   182
Charcoal or pencil line art   32–33
Charge-coupled device   85
Choke   102
Coated label papers   203
Coated printing papers   203–204
Coating   196–197
Color
  brightness   71–72
  fake   63
  flat   63
  process   63
  saturation   71–72
  spot   63
Color correction   75–76
  saturation   71–72
Color electronic prepress systems   85–87
Color perception   72–74
  Farnsworth-Munsell 100-Hue Test   73
  Ishihara test   73
Color proofing   88
Color reproduction   63–88
  additive process   66–70
  subtractive process   66–70
Color scanners, flatbed   85
Color separation   64, 81–82
Color theory   64–74
Comb binding   184
Combination folder   173–174
Common-impression press (flexographic)   143–144
Complementary flats   95–97
Composite negative and positive   98
Computer illustration   54–55
Contact frame   107–109
Continuous ink jet printing   160–163
Continuous-tone art   36
  highlights   36
  middletones   36
  shadows   36
Conventional art and copy preparation   5–45
Copy, camera-ready   31

continuous-tone   29
line   27–28
Cover papers   204–205
Cutters   185
Cylinder press (screen printing)   148–150

Desktop publishing   47
Diecutting   189–190
Digital halftones   58–61
Direct digital color proofing   88
Direct-to-plate technology   121
Dithering   60–61
Double printing   98
Drop-on-demand ink jet printing   163–164

Edge treatments   18
Electromechanical engraving   113
Electronic prepress production   5, 47–61
Electrophotography   157–160
Electrostatic plates   112
Electrostatic printing, paper requirements for   213
Embossing   186–187

Fake color   63, 101
Film assembly   89–105
   multicolor   100–101
   process-color   103–105
Film flats, complementary   98
   negative   91–94
   positive   94–95
Finishing   186–190
   diecutting   189–190
   embossing   186–187
   foil stamping   188–189
   in paper manufacture   195–196
Flat color   63
Flatbed scanner   53, 85
Flatbed screen printing press   145–148
Flats   89–95
Flexographic inks   220
Flexographic platemaking   120
Flexographic presswork   140–145
Flexography, paper requirements for   211
Flood coat   147
Foil stamping   188–189
Folding   168–174
Frequency-modulated screening   61

Gloss   197
Grain direction   198
Grammage   198
Gravure, paper requirements for   211
Gravure cylinder   113–114
Gravure inks   220
Gravure presswork   151–155
Gray balance   77
Gray component replacement   79–81
Gray scale   59–61

Halftone cell   60
Halftones, digital   58–61
Hand table   145
Hand-held scanner   53
Hand-operated screen printing tables   145–146
Head banding   182
Hue   70

Image carriers   107–121
Image register   98–99, 102–103
Ink   215–221
Ink jet printing   160–164
   paper requirements for   213
In-line press   144–145

Knife folder   169–170
Knife-cut stencils   115
Knockout   98

Layouts   7–9, 89–95
Ledger papers   205
Letterpress, paper requirements for   212–213
Letterpress inks   218
Letterpress plates   118–120
Letterpress presses   123–125
Lightweight printing papers   206
Line art   32–36
   brush and ink   32–33
   charcoal or pencil   32–33
   line conversion or posterization   34–36
   pen and ink   32–33
   shading film   34
Line conversion   34–36
Line copy   27–28
Liquid inks   219–220

Lithographic inks   218
Lithographic plates   107–112
    waterless   136–139
Lithographic presswork   125–139
Lithography, paper requirements for   209–211
Loose-leaf binding   183

Manifold and onionskin papers   206
Mechanical binding   183–185

Negative, composite   98
Negative film flats   91–94
Negative-working plate   110–111
Newspaper inks   218–219
Newsprint   206
Nonimpact printing   157–164

One-side press layouts   89
Opacity   197
Overhead scanner   53
Overlay proofs   88

Page layout, electronic   51–52
Paint programs   48–49
Paper, types of   191–213
Paper cutting   165–168
Paper machine   194–195
Paper properties   197–198
Paper weight   198–199
Parchment   206
Paste inks   217–219
Pasteup   25–31
Pen-and-ink line art   32–33
Perfect binding   176–177
Photocombining   98
Photodirect plates   111–112
Photostencil systems   115–118
Platemaking, lithographic   107–112
    bimetal   111
    negative- and positive-working   110–111
Positive, composite   98
Positive film flats   94–95
Positive-working plate   110–111
Posterization   34–36
Prepress, electronic   47–61
Prepress proofs   88
Presensitized surface plates   109–111

Press, automatic cylinder   147–148
  common-impression (flexographic)   143–144
  cylinder   148–150
  flatbed   145–148
  flatbed, letterpress   124
  in-line   144–145
  lithographic sheetfed   127–131
  lithographic web   132–136
  platen   124
  rotary   150–151
  screen printing, automatic flatbed   147–148
  stack   143
Press layouts, one-side combination   89
  one-side multiple   89
  one-up   89–90
  sheetwise   89–90
  work-and-tumble   89
  work-and-turn   89–90
Press layouts   89
Presswork   123–155
  flexographic   140–145
  gravure   151–155
  letterpress   123–125
  lithographic   125–139
  screen printing   145–151
Printer's spreads   31
Process color   63
Process-color film assembly   103–105
Process-color printing   101
Production, electronic prepress   47–61
Proofing   88
Proofreading   25, 27, 50–51
Proofs   88
Publishing, desktop   47

Reader's spreads   31
Reproduction, color   63–88
Resolution   59–61
Reverse   98
Rotary press   150–151
Rotary-drum scanners   82–85
Rotogravure presses   152–154
Rounding   180
Running heads or footers   51

Saddle-stitching   174–176
Safety papers   207

Saturation   71–72
Scaling art   37
Scanners   52–54
  flatbed   53, 85
  hand-held   53
  overhead   53
  rotary-drum   82–85
Screen printing, paper requirements for   211–212
Screen printing image carriers   114–118
Screen printing inks   219
Screen printing presswork   145–151
Screening, frequency-modulated   61
Screening, stochastic   61
Screens, multifilament mesh   118
Semiautomatic flatbed presses   146
Sewing   178–179
  McCain   178
  saddle   178
  side   178
  Smyth   178–179
Shading film   34
Sheetfed offset lithographic paper requirements   209–210
Sheetwise press layout   89–90
Side stitching   174–176
Single-color film assembly   95–99
Spelling checker   50
Spiral binding   184
Spot color   63
Spot-color printing   101
Spread   102
  printer's   31
  reader's   31
Stack press   143
Step and repeat   100
Stochastic screening   61
Stripping   89–105
Subtractive color reproduction process   66–70
Surface plates, presensitized and wipe-on   109–111
Surprint proofs   88
Surprinting   98

Tag papers   207
Text papers   207–208
Thumbnail sketches   7–8
Tissue overlay   31
Tone reproduction   76
Transfer proofs   88

Trap   102
Trimming   185–186
Type   51
Typesetting   9–25
Typography   9–25, 51

Uncoated groundwood printing papers   208
Uncoated groundwood-free printing papers   208–209
Undercolor removal   79

Vector-based programs   55
Visible spectrum   64–66

Waterless offset plate technology   136–139
Web offset lithographic paper requirements   210–211
Wedding papers   209
Wipe-on surface plates   109–111
Wire stitching   174–176
Word processing package   50
Work-and-tumble press layout   89
Work-and-turn press layout   89–90
WYSIWYG   47

About the Author

Deborah L. Stevenson has been an assistant editor in the Technical Information Group at GATF since 1987. She has managed several textbook projects in that time including *What the Printer Should Know about Paper, What the Printer Should Know about Ink,* and *Printing Plant Layout and Facility Design.* Ms. Stevenson has also contributed material to *GATFWORLD,* the Foundation's bimonthly technical magazine, assisted in production of the ninth edition of *The Lithographers Manual,* and cowrote the script and checklist for GATF's *Selecting a School for a Career in Graphic Communications: An Industry with Vision* videotape presentation.